Greenhill
Books

HOSTAGE
RESCUE
MANUAL

HOSTAGE RESCUE MANUAL

TACTICS OF THE COUNTER-TERRORIST PROFESSIONALS

Leroy Thompson

GREENHILL BOOKS, LONDON
STACKPOLE BOOKS, PENNSYLVANIA

Greenhill Books

Hostage Rescue Manual: Tactics of the Counter-Terrorist Professionals first published 2001 by
Greenhill Books, Lionel Leventhal Limited, Park House,
1 Russell Gardens, London NW11 9NN
www.greenhillbooks.com
and
Stackpole Books, 5067 Ritter Road, Mechanicsburg, PA 17055, USA

British Library Cataloguing in Publication Data
Thompson, Leroy
Hostage rescue manual
1. Hostage negotiations – Handbooks, manuals, etc. 2. Rescues – Handbooks, manuals,
etc.
I. Title
355.4'1

ISBN 1-85367-472-9

Library of Congress Cataloging-in-Publication Data available

Designed by John Anastasio, Creative Line, 1 Mercer Street, London WC2H 9QJ

Printed and bound in Great Britain by Butler & Tanner Ltd, Frome and London

Contents

List of Plates

Appearing between pages 113 and 128

Preface

When hostages are taken, the incident evokes a combination of horror and empathy among a country's population. At the same time, unless a response is carefully planned and successfully carried out, a government can appear impotent or non-responsive to the dangers facing its citizens. Often, the details of hostage incidents are kept from the press and the population to protect the hostages and those tasked with saving them. As a result, though incidents may end through negotiation or through armed action by security elements, only the sketchiest details of how the operation was carried out are normally available.

In this work I've attempted to assemble a guide through the process of hostage rescue both for men and women who work in security-related fields and those who want to understand better the missions and skills of those who silently protect society from those who would use the threat to innocents to extort concessions. Much of the information contained in this work is based on my own experience in training hostage rescue units in various parts of the world, while other information is based on standard operating procedures of some of the most successful international, national, state and local SWAT or Tactical Teams.

It must be borne in mind, however, that rescue tactics and standard operating procedures will differ greatly from country to country based upon form of government, culture, religion and myriad other factors. In some countries, for example, hostages of a certain race, sex, or caste might be considered more valuable hostages than others. Even in democracies, where theoretically all are equal, a rich, influential hostage will naturally be expected by hostage-takers to prompt a significant response from authorities and the media. Cultural influences may also play an important part in how an incident transpires. For example, at least one incident in the United States was resolved because the leader of the hostage-takers was disconcerted by the necessity of performing bodily functions in close proximity to the hostages. His fastidiousness influenced him to end the incident peacefully and more quickly than would have been likely otherwise. (For a synopsis of actual incidents referred to throughout the text, please see Appendix 1.)

The differences in police authority will also influence the handling of a hostage incident. In Great Britain where only a limited number of police are armed, for example, it may take longer to have armed containment personnel on the scene, though the use of armed response vehicles has allowed a much faster response than formerly. On the other hand, the weapons culture in the United States is such that as many as 50% of homes contain firearms of some kind. The likelihood of encountering an armed suspect in a 'hostage' or 'barricade' situation is therefore much greater than in the UK and US HR units train accordingly, placing greater emphasis on the need to secure a site on entry and confront – rather than simply contain – the terrorist.

The issue of investment prompts further distinctions in practice. It may be surprising to the layman to learn that one of the largest markets for HR work is occupied by smaller teams with tight budgets, who are often tasked with maximising the limited resources to which they have access. At the other extreme, wealthier countries with highly trained police or military rescue units will be more likely to have access to the most modern and most sophisticated equipment and weapons, as well as intensive training programmes.

The more authoritarian the government, generally the more likely there will be pressure on response units to act quickly to end the incident to prevent the perception of the government as weak. More democratic governments, on the other hand, will be under pressure to place great emphasis on the lives of the hostages.

As a result, the tactics I have presented in this work are by no means the only ones which have been or are being used by hostage rescue units. I do feel that the tactics and procedures included in this work offer a sound basic understanding of the steps necessary to plan and implement a successful rescue. It must be remembered, too, that tactics for rescuing hostages will continue to evolve as equipment, weapons and threats evolve. Highly specialised and classified techniques will not be included in this volume of work.

I have endeavoured to help the reader understand that a successful hostage rescue operation is a mosaic composed of many skills and many individuals, each of vital importance. While the negotiator attempts to use his empathy and understanding of psychology to end an incident peacefully, he is also gathering intelligence which may assist an entry team if they are needed. Through technological and other means, intelligence experts are constantly upgrading and updating their intelligence about the hostage-taker, hostages and site. Silently observing the incident, preparing to end it with one precision shot if necessary, are the snipers and observers. Meanwhile, the entry team – the men in black wearing gas masks and carrying submachine guns – refine their plan in case they are called upon to provide the 'final option'.

From the initial establishment of a perimeter to contain a hostage incident, until its successful conclusion through negotiation, the 'green light' order to a sniper, or a dynamic entry, the Hostage Rescue Manual allows the reader to follow the progress of a hostage rescue incident in detail.

Leroy Thompson, St. Louis, Missouri, 2001

Glossary

Ammo	Ammunition
Ammo	Ammunition
BDU	US military camouflage
BTSP	Boat Tail Soft Point
CAD	Computer Assisted Drafting
CP	Command Post
Delta Force	US Army counterterrorist unit
EMT	Emergency Medical Technicians
EOD	Explosive Ordnance Disposal
FBI	Federal Bureau of Investigation
FBI HRT	FBI Hostage Rescue Team
GIGN	Groupe d'Intervention Gendarmerie Nationale (French Counterterrorist unit under Ministry of Defence)
GSG-9	Grenzschutzgruppe 9 (German counterterrorist unit drawn from the border guards)
HazMat	Hazardous materials
HRU	Hostage Rescue Unit
K9	Dogs trained for military or police use
LTR	Light Tactical Rifle
MOA	Minute Of Angle
MOPP	Mission Oriented Protective Posture
NATO	North Atlantic Treaty Organisation
NBC	Nuclear, Biological or Chemical
RAID	Reaction, Assistance, Intervention, Dissuader (French Counterterrorist unit under Ministry of the Interior)
Recce	Recconaisance
SAS	Special Air Service
SBS	Special Boat Service (British special forces under the Royal Marines)
SEAL Team Six	US Navy counterterrorist unit
SERT	Special Emergency Response Team
SIG	Swiss manufacturer of small arms
SMG	Submachine gun
SOCOM	Special Operations Command
SOPs	Standard Operating Procedures
SRT	Special Response Teams
SSG	Steyr sniping rifle
SWAT	Special Weapons and Tactics Teams
TOC	Tactical Operations Centre
TAP	Tactical Application Police
USMC	United States Marine Corps
Zodiac	Rubber boats used by military and police units

CONTAINING THE INCIDENT AND ESTABLISHING A PERIMETER

Hostage situations may arise from a variety of initial incidents. Among the most common are domestic violence or divorce, an interrupted crime, terrorism, an attempted arrest, or 'suicide by cop'.

In the suicide by cop scenario, the hostage-taker may use the hostages as a ploy to force police to shoot him or her. Frequently, however, in such situations, the hostage-taker changes his mind at some point and may kill hostages in an attempt to avoid being killed or captured or he may decide that to ensure that police will shoot him he must either kill a hostage or a police officer. The interrupted crime scenario will usually arise when robbers are caught within the bank, business, etc. they are attempting to rob by responding police officers.

In this situation, the criminals take hostages in an attempt to force authorities to let them get away.

THE INITIAL RESPONSE

In each of these situations, police patrol officers will normally be the first on the scene. Upon arrival, if the hostage-taker is not actually shooting people at the time, responding officers should attempt to contain the incident by setting up a perimeter which will keep the hostage-taker or -takers contained and innocent bystanders from wandering into the area. Initially, the first officers on the scene will try to take up positions which allow them to observe as much of the area around the site as possible; then, as additional officers arrive, gaps in the perimeter may be filled in. K-9 officers can be especially valuable in setting up an initial perimeter and later in manning an outer perimeter.

CONTAINING SUSPECTS AND HOSTAGES

It is extremely important to keep the hostage-taker and hostages from 'going mobile' if possible. That is, try to avoid allowing the hostage-taker to enter a vehicle with the hostage or to take a driver hostage and force him or her to drive away. It is also important during the setting of the initial perimeter to retain any witnesses who might be on the scene so that they may be questioned to gain intelligence about the hostage-takers, the hostages and the venue in which the hostage-taker has gone to ground.

The four basic precepts which govern the initial response to a hostage incident are:

1 **CONTAIN** – remove the hostage-taker's mobility.

2 **CONTROL** – limit the hostage-taker's movements as well as the movements of those who might attempt to enter the area.

3 **COMMUNICATE** – establish contact with the hostage-taker at the earliest opportunity. However, actual negotiations should wait for a trained hostage negotiator.

4 **COORDINATE** – begin evaluating what other assets will be necessary to resolve the incident (i.e., SWAT personnel, emergency medical team, fire department, hostage negotiator, media relations person, etc.).

ARE HOSTAGES PRESENT?

One of the most important pieces of information, which can be gleaned early in an incident, is whether there are or are not hostages. Once the presence or absence of hostages has been determined, then the response can be planned based on whether authorities are facing a hostage or barricade situation. While setting up the initial perimeter, it may be necessary to evacuate nearby residents who might be injured by gunfire. The first officers on the scene should also develop a quick contingency plan in case the hostage-taker starts killing hostages or attempts to leave with a hostage. This plan will often be as simple as designating officers who will enter the building and attempt to stop a shooter. However, since patrol officers normally lack heavier body armour and heavier weapons such an entry carries the potential for substantial casualties.

DEALING WITH ACTIVE SHOOTERS

Although some agencies have standard operating procedures (SOPs) covering the responsibilities of those initially responding to a hostage or barricade incident, it is also necessary to be prepared to deal with an 'active shooter', as many who carry out armed attacks in schools, post offices or other heavily populated buildings have been termed. Agencies which have SWAT personnel who are assigned to patrol duties when not on a callout may find that a few trained officers are on the scene, possibly with their special equipment in their vehicles. In this case, these officers can prepare for an entry if immediate action appears necessary to save lives. An important initial decision, however, is: what are the consequences of taking action? of not taking action?

SLOWING THINGS DOWN

It also important to remember that time is an important element in defusing a hostage situation. Normally, the first thirty minutes are very critical in barricade or hostage situations because that is when the hostage-taker/shooter is most excited. That is why initial containment is so important. The normal rule of thumb is: the longer an incident lasts, the more likely it will be settled without violence. Therefore, unless hostages or bystanders are being killed, once the incident is contained, the initial responders should try to slow things down until SWAT and a negotiator are on the scene.

ESTABLISING A TIGHT PERIMETER

Setting up a tight perimeter as soon as possible serves many useful purposes. It removes control from the hostage-taker and maybe help to convince him to negotiate. A tight perimeter also prevents family and friends of the hostage-taker interfering, a problem in some domestic hostage situations. It also prevents the hostage-taker from taking additional hostages. When establishing the perimeter, leave a reactionary gap to give officers room to manoeuvre and a chance to react to a hostile suspect attempting to exit.

THE INNER AND OUTER PERIMETERS

When enough officers are on the scene an inner and an outer perimeter will be established.

PLACEMENT

It is especially important that officers on the inner perimeter should try to find protection which gives cover but also allows them to observe doors and windows where the hostage-taker might appear. These officers should also be careful that they are not placing themselves in a position to be caught in crossfire between other officers and the hostage-taker. Knowing what weapons the hostage-

taker has can help officers determine what type of cover is appropriate and whether they need to establish the outer perimeter further back, as in situations where the shooter is armed with a rifle.

THE INNER AND OUTER PERIMETER TEAMS

Normally, as soon as specially trained SWAT, TAC or other entry/hostage rescue personnel are on the scene they will take over the inner perimeter. Once they are in position, they will assume the primary responsibility for containing the hostage-takers and will immediately plot ranges should the subjects opt to 'go mobile'. The outer perimeter team will deal with bystanders, the press and other outsiders. If an entry team is deployed to 'go in' then the inner perimeter team can give covering fire while this team is moving into position. The inner perimeter team will often be in charge of deploying chemical weapons such as tear gas. When those manning the perimeter are law enforcement personnel or military police it is important to remember that at some point the venue of the hostage incident will probably be considered a crime scene. As a result, perimeter personnel must be prepared to secure the area for crime scene technicians at the conclusion of an incident.

THE BRIEF

Inner perimeter personnel must be fully briefed so that all are aware of certain basic operational procedures. They must know the rules of engagement and the positions of all other personnel on the perimeter so that they can establish fields of fire.   They must also be aware of the suspects' armament and position so they can assess their own danger of taking fire. Perimeter personnel should constantly monitor their radios. While modern communications equipment generates very little noise, if restricted to older equipment the volume should be sufficiently low to be inaudible to the hostage-

taker, who might otherwise learn about SWAT movement or tactical operations.

EXAMPLE
Radio noise can also be a problem. For example, a Detroit SRT member was killed when a senior commander approached the scene with her radio turned up, thus compromising the element of surprise.

Unless relieved or so ordered, no perimeter personnel should leave their positions. Once the entry team carries out an entry, perimeter personnel should not be authorised to fire their weapons unless it is necessary to save a life. Finally, it must be emphasised that movement around the incident site should be carried out using cover and concealment. A route should be planned in advance. It should be borne in mind that the shortest route to a position may not be the safest. In some situations other personnel will cover while an officer moves into position. During movement at night, it is important to be aware of back lighting which can silhouette personnel.

THE COMMAND POST

As soon as the ranking military or police officer who will be the incident commander arrives on the scene, he should find a command post and stay there so that he can be easily located. It may be advisable at this point to begin setting up a tactical operations center (TOC) or command post (CP) to coordinate intelligence and maintain contact with the various elements on the scene.

LOCATION OF CP
This CP should be located close enough to the action that command personnel can visually inspect the scene and retain close contact with officers on the scene yet far enough away that they are not likely to take fire. Many larger agencies have a mobile command post which can be quickly

brought to the scene of an emergency or incident. Such mobile CPs are very useful as they already contain telephones, televisions, briefing materials and various other items.

AUTHOR'S NOTE
To prevent them giving away information about SWAT operations, the press should be kept away form the command post.

MANNING THE CP
There are two schools of thought about incorporating hostage negotiators and those who will make the decision about authorising the use of snipers or entry teams in the same CP. There is the possibility, especially with inexperienced negotiators, that they will inadvertently give away an impending assault by a change in voice or manner if they are aware that the teams are 'going in'. On the other hand, the negotiator is an invaluable source of intelligence and can help distract the hostage-taker during an entry or lure him into position for a sniper to take a shot. One solution is to have the negotiator in the same CP,

but in a separate room from those planning the assault.

ROLE OF THE INCIDENT COMMANDER

The incident commander needs to identify the key elements of the situation and decide if special personnel and equipment will be needed. Additionally, he should make sure that the perimeter is set and press and bystanders are being kept at a safe distance.

The incident commander will also need to assemble knowledgeable advisors such as the hostage negotiator, SWAT commander and fire marshal (the official in the US fire department who checks public buildings for safety) or others who have knowledge of the area in which the hostages are held. As soon as possible, too, the incident commander needs to assess realistically the capabilities of the personnel at his disposal to determine if he needs to request assistance from state or federal police or military special units. He will need to begin development of

a simple yet flexible plan as early as possible in case the hostage-taker begins killing hostages, or other events necessitate immediate action.

As soon as enough personnel are on the scene, the commander needs to chose competent subordinates and delegate responsibilities. One important choice will be a public information officer to deal with the press so that the commander may remain focused on the incident. Those in the command element must also arrange for simple necessities such as the availability of food and water and toilet facilities for personnel manning the perimeter and for SWAT personnel.

THE INTERMEDIATE PHASE

During the intermediate stage of a hostage incident, it is important to 'tie down' the phone lines going into the scene as soon as possible so only the authorities can talk with the hostage-taker. This aspect will be discussed in more detail in

Chapter 3 on hostage negotiations. During the early and intermediate stage of an incident, it is possible that hostages or others will escape from, or be released from, the building. In this case, it is important to treat them with care to be sure they really have been released or have escaped and are not one of the hostage-takers attempting to leave the scene. Once their identities have been established, released or escaped hostages must be thoroughly debriefed for any intelligence they can give.

As SWAT personnel take over the inner perimeter, then officers who had been occupying those positions are available to augment outer perimeter personnel or to return to patrol duties. As the incident progresses, the outer perimeter personnel will have to watch the press to make sure no one has attempted to move closer to the incident and also to make sure they are not filming preparations by SWAT which might compromise a rescue operation.

Although the black-clad entry team member, the precision tactical marksman or the tireless hostage negotiator are the most recognisable elements of the team attempting to resolve a hostage incident, it is important to remember that the containment and security provided by those personnel manning the perimeter allow the other elements of a hostage rescue team to operate.

INTELLIGENCE

CHAPTER 2

Intelligence is invaluable in dealing with a hostage situation. For both the entry team which may have to go in to resolve the incident with gunfire, or the negotiator attempting to end the incident without violence, intelligence can make the difference between a successful conclusion to the incident and a tragic one.

CRITICAL INTELLIGENCE

Critical intelligence in a hostage incident can include information on:

- the hostage-takers
- hostage-takers' criminal and medical histories
- hostage-takers' mind sets
- hostages
- number of hostages
- why the hostage-takers have taken the hostages
- hostage-takers' propensity towards violence
- weapons
- layout of the building
- barricades or booby traps in place
- best entry route and as much other useful data as possible.

For the information gathered to become useful intelligence it must be:

- Timely.
- Relevant.
- Accurate.
- Refined.
- Communicated to those who need it.

Timeliness is extremely important. A hostage-taker who has indicated he will kill a hostage within five minutes has imposed time limits on the response which may dictate that snipers will be given the order to 'take him out' or that an entry team will be given the 'go' order.

Likewise, the information must be **relevant** to the actual event. The fact that a suspect was a demolitions expert in the army is important because it might indicate the likelihood of explosives being present, while the fact that he likes a certain rock group might offer a piece of useful information to the negotiator but is certainly less relevant.

That information is **accurate** is obviously of absolute importance. If members of an entry team are told that all of the hostages are in a certain room, they must be confident that they can focus on clearing that room as rapidly as possible.

EXAMPLE

A good example of the problems with inaccurate intelligence occurred during the SAS assault at Princes Gate (see Appendix 1). Frame charges were used on the windows of the embassy by Pagoda units, which created a new hazard: fire from the curtains. The SAS had no substantial fire-proof kit at this time. They were also unaware that one interior doorway they had planned to use had been blocked and was unusable. As a result, though

accurate intelligence is the goal, plans must remain flexible to allow for some of the data on which a plan has been based proving incorrect.

Refinement of information is the job of the intelligence specialist or specialists in the CP. They must sort which facts are of importance from the mass of information which they will be accumulating.

Most of all, intelligence needs to be **communicated** to those who need it. If a sniper/observer team notices the hostage-taker leaving the hostages alone for a moment, he must immediately communicate this fact as it may influence an entry or an order for him to take a shot. Likewise, if a negotiator learns something from background noise or from the hostage-taker, he or she should immediately write the information down and pass it to the intelligence analyst.

USING FAMILIAR CONTACTS

Useful intelligence about the hostage-taker or -takers may be gleaned from many sources, including family members of the hostage-taker or takers, co-workers, neighbours, bystanders, police officers who have previously encountered the individual, initial response officers, mail carriers, UPS drivers or other delivery personnel and other observers. The hostage-taker's criminal records, hospital records, military discharge, school records or employee records may also offer useful data.

THE HOSTAGE-TAKER'S CRIMINAL AND MEDICAL HISTORIES

In assessing the likelihood of the hostage-taker committing a violent act, there are various factors which must be evaluated. These can include mental disorders such as schizophrenia or mood disorders such as depression. Paranoid schizophrenia or Bipolar Disorder may indicate an even greater propensity towards violence. A history of substance abuse may also be an indicator of potential violence, especially if combined with one of the mental disorders.

Among indicators of increased risk of short term violence are:

- hostile suspiciousness,
- agitation and excitement,
- disturbed thinking, including disorganisation and unusual thoughts, and
- command hallucinations (voices telling the subject to take hostile action against people).

Among other factors which must be considered in evaluating the subject's likelihood of taking violent action against the hostages are factors such as:

age, since younger subjects are normally more prone to violence; **sex,** as men are normally considered more likely to commit violent acts; **IQ,** as those with lower intelligence offer a greater risk of violent behaviour. Also: lower socioeconomic level; job instability and employment problems; gang membership; a history of sadistic behaviour; and a history of negative contact with law enforcement. In some cases an anniversary of some significant emotional event (i.e., the date of a divorce) may act as a trigger to violence. A history of violence, particularly sadistic violence, is a particularly good predictor.

THE HOSTAGE-TAKER'S MIND-SET

Other predictors may come through the hostage-taker's observed actions towards hostages. If the hostage-taker continually menaces the hostage, points weapons at him or her and talks to the authorities or negotiator about harming the hostage, these all may indicate a greater likelihood of taking violent action. The negotiator must be trained to evaluate the hostage-taker's mood and to alert the incident commander to growing irrationality or talk of dying and taking the hostage and/or police with him. The psychological profile of the hostage-taker can be a useful predictor if carefully assembled, especially if the team has access to a trained psychiatrist or psychologist who can assist in evaluating the hostage-taker's behaviour. Many hostage rescue teams have developed standardised forms to organise information about hostage-takers and hostages (see Appendix 2).

AUTHOR'S NOTE

The author has found it is a good idea to print the hostage and hostage-taker profile forms on different coloured paper to facilitate quick identification.

WORKING OUT THE BASICS

As soon as possible, at a minimum the following information is needed about the hostage-takers:

- How many are there?
- Who are they?
- Who is their leader?
- How many are male/female?
- What is their ethnic background?
- What are their descriptions?
- Are there photos of them?
- What is their state of mind?
- What is their armament?
- Do they have ballistic vests?
- Have they deployed booby traps/explosives?
- Do they have gas masks?
- What are they asking for?

There are also basic questions about hostages to be answered as soon as possible:

- How many are there?
- How many male/female?
- Who are they?
- Are there psychological profiles of the hostages predicting behaviour?
- What are their descriptions?
- What are they wearing?
- Do any hostages have special medical problems?
- How are they being held?

The psychological profile can become quite important in an extended incident. For example, when the Royal Dutch Marines launched their assault against a hi-jacked train, their psychological profiles correctly predicted the hostages most likely to panic and jump up during the assault.

AUTHOR'S NOTE

With regard to the hostages' clothing, it is important to be aware that more sophisticated hostage-takers have been known to switch clothing with the hostages.

THE SCENE OF THE INCIDENT

Information about the site of the incident is as important as information about the hostages and hostage-takers.

Data needs to be assembled about:

- Premises: office, home, retail establishment, government building, factory, etc.
- Number of entry points: doors, windows, sewers, vents.
- Doors: made of what? do they open in or out? types of locks/hinges?
- Building construction: brick or frame?
- Where the hostage-taker is believed to be in the building.
- Who knows the site, has blueprints, keys, etc.
- Terrain around the site.
- Are there flammable or explosive materials in the building?
- Utilities: point of entry into site
- Are there external lights, especially with motion detectors?
- Is there an alarm system?

EXAMPLE

In one instance an FBI SWAT team's stealth approach to a residence was compromised by security lights coming on. The team was forced into a dynamic entry because of the loss of surprise, and one team member was killed in the process of carrying out that entry. Some teams have suppressed .22 pistols or rifles specifically to deal with lights which may compromise an approach.

MAKING A SKETCH OF THE SITE

It is important that a member of the SWAT team who is aware of the details about the site which will be most useful in planning an assault is sent to recce the site and sketch it. Included in this sketch should be possible concealment points for assault team members such as fences, bushes, corners, etc.. When sketching buildings, label features in a standard manner to allow information to be relayed over the radio quickly and confidentially. One common method is to use

colour codes for the four sides of the structure, then a number for each storey from top down and a number for each window or door from left to right.   The reason the storeys are numbered from top down is that many buildings, due to construction on a hill, have a different number of storeys on different sides. By using the top-down method, everyone will remain consistent about which level is under discussion (see Diagram 2.1).

2.1 COMMUNICATION CODE FOR BUILDINGS

So that entry teams, snipers, perimeter personnel, and others involved in a hostage incident may be consistent when referring to a building, it is useful to have a code such as the one illustrated. If a hostage-taker were spotted at the front, on the second floor, it could be broadcast as: Suspect at white, 3/3.

24

Sketches should illustrate doors, windows, utility hookups, fences and as many other details as possible. Label types of windows and doors (i.e., single, double, sliding, storm, etc. and which way they open). From witnesses and others make sketches of the interior. In office buildings, it is important to note if windows are mirrored or tinted as it will be necessary to deploy high intensity lights shining inward to allow a sniper any chance of a shot.

Find out if there are other apartments, condos, houses, offices or classrooms with similar layouts. Take photographs whenever possible.

In many public buildings, fire regulations will require the posting on each level of a floor plan which shows the layout.

It is often possible to deduce quite a bit about a residence from windows. For example, the largest ones with fancier curtains indicate living areas, middle-sized ones usually indicate bedrooms and small ones next to bedrooms usually indicate bathrooms.

Many SWAT teams now have Computer Assisted Drafting (CAD) programs on lap top computers which allow them to prepare a site plan quickly and run copies for team members.

EXAMPLE

Teams also often do site surveys, in advance, of sites such as courthouses, schools, hospitals and airports where a hostage situation may arise. However, no one can predict in advance where an incident might take place. For example, one FBI SWAT team found itself faced with a hostage incident taking place in the local FBI offices.

ELECTRONIC DEVICES

Information about what is transpiring within the site of a hostage incident may also be gained using various types of electronic devices. Endoscopes may be introduced through walls or vent systems to observe the hostage-takers, while transmitters, laser beams, chimney microphones or electronic stethoscopes may be used to listen to what is being said within a site.

These and other intelligence gathering devices will be discussed in more detail in Chapter 6 on specialised equipment.

EVALUATING TERRAIN AROUND THE SITE

In looking at the terrain around the site, five main considerations will normally be most important.

1 **What are the key terrain features?** Look at those which will give the SWAT team and authorities the most advantage and will also prevent escape of the hostage-takers. Although high ground is normally desirable to allow deployment of snipers or to allow observation posts, there are situations when the more advantageous positions will not be above the site. Often, there will be a gully, culvert or some other feature below ground level which is important because it allows a covert approach but would also offer a good escape route for suspects.

2 **As already mentioned terrain which allows good observation points is critical.** Care must also be taken to choose terrain which allows good fields of fire for hostage rescue personnel, both snipers and containment teams.

3 **Evaluate terrain for cover and concealment.** Cover should be defined as those features which actually provide protection against small arms fire from the hostage-takers, while concealment may be defined as those features which hide the presence or movement of the hostage rescue team.

4 **Obstacles presented by terrain should be carefully evaluated and noted in case it is necessary to launch a rescue attempt.** Obstacles not only include fences, hedges, ditches and other physical features, but also include security lights, alarm systems and attack dogs.

5 **In evaluating terrain look for all possible avenues of approach or avenues of escape.** In looking at the avenues of escape, they should be considered as routes which should be interdicted to prevent the escape of hostage-takers, but they may also be considered as retreat routes if an assault has to be aborted.

In the TOC or CP, the intelligence analyst should organise information by areas to make it easier to disseminate to the actual operators.

A typical breakdown might include information about:

- hostage-takers
- hostages
- site
- weapons and ammo in the hands of the suspects
- demands
  a) current
  b) lowered
  c) raised
- floor plans
- utilities
- medical problems

EQUIPMENT ON SITE

Often, a bulletin board or blackboard will be devoted to each major area of intelligence. This information needs to be constantly updated and the most current information prepared for the snipers, entry team, command personnel and negotiator. This information will be used in adjusting the entry plan.

Facilities, such as a high quality photocopier, which allows copies and enlargements of photos of hostage-takers, hostages and the site to be made quickly are also important.

ROLE OF PERSONNEL

Personnel at the tactical operations centre should also attempt to locate an area which duplicates the actual site as much as possible, for the entry teams to use for practice. However, this area needs to be close by so the team is available. In some cases taping off a nearby parking lot is the best that can be done. If, however, the incident takes place in a multi-storey building, it may be possible to practise in offices or apartments on another floor which duplicate the one in which the hostages are being held. As the intelligence is updated, command personnel must constantly evaluate whether they need specialised equipment or personnel. For example, if there are indicators that explosive devices have been placed, then an Explosive Ordnance Disposal (EOD) team will have to be alerted and brought to the scene.

OPERATIONAL SECURITY

There is a tendency, in considering intelligence for tactical operations such as hostage rescue, to think that counterintelligence is not as critical as it is in military operations. This may not, however, be the case. The press or, in terrorist incidents, accomplices of the hostage-takers may be highly desirous of obtaining information about rescue plans. Obviously, information gained by the hostage-takers might enable them to counter a move by hostage rescue elements. As a result, basic operational security should be practised around the TOC/CP.

Basic operational security can be broken into five steps:

1 Identify sensitive information by analysing the elements of preparations, knowledge of which could prove beneficial to the opposition.

2 Identify the threat by considering who would value from this information.

3 Identify vulnerabilities by looking at who or what might give away critical information; this could include support services, the press, civilians watching an entry team practise, voices in the background when the negotiator has the hostage-taker on the line, etc.

4 Conduct a risk assessment.

5 Establish countermeasures for those risks identified. For example, to make sure that nothing important is overheard while the hostage negotiator is on the line with the hostage-taker, keep other personnel in a separate room.

PLANNING THE MISSION

Once intelligence is gathered, it should be used for operational planning. An assault plan will normally continue to evolve as intelligence is gained right up to the point at which the team is sent in.

Normally, the priority will be:

1 The lives of the hostages.

2 Then the lives of other innocent civilians.

3 Then the lives of police or military personnel.

4 Finally, the lives of the hostage-takers.

The operational plan itself will often be in military format and broken into five primary categories:

1 **SITUATION.** This portion of the plan will include information about how the incident arose, the hostage-takers and hostages, terrain and other relevant details.

2 **MISSION.** It is important at this point to delineate exactly what the most critical portion of the mission is. Although normally the primary mission is to rescue the hostages, there might be exceptions. At a nuclear facility, for example, assuring the integrity and security of the installation might well take precedence over the hostages under the 'Good of the many, versus the good of the few' precept. Part of the mission might be to recover some item in the possession of the hostage-takers (i.e., classified information). For police teams, arresting the suspects and securing the crime scene might be part of the mission. In special circumstances, killing the subject could be part of the mission; if, for example, he had in his hand on a detonator for an explosive device and this was the only way to stop him.

3 **EXECUTION.** This part of the plan delineates exactly how the mission will be accomplished, though it is important also to include methods of dealing with contingencies.

4 **ADMINISTRATION AND LOGISTICS.** This part of the plan lays out what equipment and personnel are needed to accomplish the mission.

5 **COMMAND/SIGNALS.** This part of the plan sets forth the chain of command, including who has authority to order the assault or to give the snipers the order to shoot. It will also list radio frequencies to be used and any radio codes which will apply.

Though having a clear operational plan is essential, the plan must not be so inflexible that it prevents personnel actually on the ground from adjusting to contingencies.

CHAPTER 3

HOSTAGE NEGOTIATION

The hostage negotiator's primary mission is to bring the hostage situation to a peaceful end by communicating with the hostage-taker and establishing a rapport. In most hostage situations, negotiation is the alternative to capitulation or the use of force. Negotiation also allows the entry team time to prepare itself should the use of force prove necessary.

FUNDAMENTALS OF SUCCESSFUL NEGOTIATION

The two primary methods of hostage negotiation have sometimes been summarised as overwhelming and boring the hostage-taker with petty decisions and details until he gives up or stalling until an entry can take place. Both are oversimplifications and, in fact, a good negotiator may well attempt to keep the hostage-taker occupied with a mass of minor decisions, while also allowing the SWAT team to prepare for a dynamic entry. Certainly, early in an incident the negotiator tries to slow things down to diffuse the danger. By keeping the hostage-taker talking, the negotiator then has a much better chance of keeping the hostages alive.

AUTHOR'S NOTE

Perhaps the best indication of the importance of the hostage negotiator can be gleaned from a 1997 study by a SWAT team in one of the largest cities in the US which found that 80% of hostage incidents were resolved through negotiation.

PHASES

During the process of hostage negotiation, the FBI has identified three phases which often occur.

1 **Opening Gambit.** This phase includes the early hours when the negotiator must calm the hostage-takers to ensure the safety of the hostages and must begin to discuss realistic demands.

2 **Jockeying for Position.** During this phase the negotiator attempts to reduce the hostage-takers' demands, perhaps achieve the release of some hostages, build rapport and look for ways of ending the situation.

3 **Endgame.** In this final phase, the hostage-taker will often become impatient and demand that things happen (i.e., his transportation to the airport and a waiting plane be provided); tension may rise. During this phase it is critical that the negotiator keeps a lid on the situation.

CONCESSIONS

Throughout the process the negotiator should make no concessions without receiving something in return. For example, if the hostage-taker wishes to speak to the media, he has to release a hostage. Many things are negotiable during an incident. These include food, drink, transportation, comfort items and utilities which have been turned off. Items which are normally not negotiable include alcohol or drugs, which might increase a hostage-taker's propensity towards

irrational action; weapons; or a hostage exchange. Although in films, it is quite common for the hero bravely to offer himself in a hostage exchange, in general, this is a bad policy. In fact, such an exchange might well convince the hostage-taker that he now has a more valuable hostage thus causing him to become more intractable.

ADAPTING

The skilled negotiator must be capable of using different approaches to fit the situation and hostage-taker. At times, he or she must be calm and helpful, while at other times the negotiator may have to become forceful to take control of the situation. Throughout the negotiations, too, the negotiator becomes the conduit through which information is filtered to the hostage-taker. As a result, the negotiator must be very astute in choosing what to convey and what to withhold. If, for example, someone is wounded during the initial stages of the hostage incident and later dies, it is probably better not to tell the hostage-taker he is a murderer, since, knowing he will face life imprisonment or the death penalty, he will have less incentive to cooperate towards a peaceful conclusion to the incident.

For negotiations to be carried out successfully, the FBI has concluded that the following preconditions are required:

- **Hostage-taker's desire to live.** With certain terrorist groups, especially those of the Shi'ite sect, the desire to die for a cause may actually outweigh the desire to live, making negotiations very problematical.

- **Sufficient force to threaten the life of the hostage-taker.** The potential for sending in a SWAT team to kill the hostage-taker gives the negotiator leverage. In at least one incident involving the IRA just knowing the SAS was on the scene brought out the barricaded suspects. On the other hand, the Dutch government had such a reputation for benevolence, that the South Moluccan terrorists who had taken over the Depunt train refused to believe that the Dutch would

resort to force, thus making negotiations difficult and finally forcing an assault by the Royal Dutch Marines (see Appendix 1).

- **Communication between the hostage-taker and the negotiator**

- **Someone with the power to make decisions for the hostage-takers**

- **One or more demands by the hostage-takers**

- **Lack of freedom of movement by the hostage-takers through containment**

- **Time to allow rapport to be established between the negotiator and the hostage-takers, as well as between the hostage-takers and the hostages**

- **A negotiator who can convey that force is available if needed but who seems willing to help the hostage-takers reach a peaceful resolution**

The fact that the negotiations may fill needs for different types of hostage-takers aids the negotiation process. For example, the criminal may see the negotiations as a way to save his life and perhaps make a deal with the authorities. The mentally ill hostage-taker will be allowed to draw attention to his problems. Finally, the terrorist may see the negotiation process as a way to further his agenda by helping him reach an audience. For many terrorists, too, the negotiation process allows them a chance to survive, perhaps to strike another day.

IDENTIFYING PROGRESS

Throughout an incident, the negotiator should watch for indicators that progress is being made in the negotiations.

Such indicators might include:

- no deaths or injuries after the negotiation process began;

- reduced threats from the subject;

- a relatively calm demeanour on the part of the subject;

- rational discussion and actions on the part of the subject;

- deadlines have passed without the subject taking action;

- more willingness on the part of the subject to bargain;

- lowered demands from the subject;

- hostages have been released;

- the negotiator feels that a rapport has developed with the subject;

- expressions of concern about the welfare of the hostages have been made by the subject;

- there are indications the subject is considering surrender.

THE NEGOTIATOR IN ACTION

In order to perform his or her function, the negotiator should project a neutral and calming persona, must focus on the practicalities of resolving the incident, must avoid becoming involved in political or philosophical disputes with the hostage-takers and must establish rapport with the terrorist leader or principal hostage-taker.

PERSONAL QUALITIES

An important skill is 'active listening', which allows a show of concern for the hostages' well-being and the hostage-taker's feelings. The negotiator must be able to narrow the discussion and focus on talking the hostage-taker out. The most successful negotiators are usually good interviewers who also have the ability to sell the hostage-taker on surrendering. Though empathy is an important characteristic, the negotiator must avoid becoming emotionally involved with the hostage-taker/s.

EXAMPLE

Studies have shown that good negotiators are normally good verbally, have self-confidence, possess good reasoning ability and show sensitivity to others.

NEGOTIATION TECHNIQUES

Good negotiators follow a strategy designed to wrest control of the incident from the hostage-takers and to defuse the likelihood of violence.

Among the techniques used by negotiators are the following:

1 Overwhelm the hostage-taker with detail: For example, if he asks for cigarettes, discuss in detail what brand and whether filter or non-filter. By keeping the hostage-taker immersed in detail, it keeps him from focusing on the hostages as much.

2 Ask open-ended questions to encourage a dialogue.

3 Avoid confrontation.

4 Try to get the hostage-taker to forget deadlines by talking through them.

5 Control access to the hostage-taker.

6 Try to gain release of groups of hostages. Sometimes this may be accomplished as a trade for access to the media or something else the hostage-taker desires. It may also be possible to convince the hostage-taker to free women, children, or those who have medical problems out of 'humanitarian' concerns or just to make it easier on him to control fewer hostages.

7 **Manipulate the hostage-taker's environment.** By controlling the electricity, phone, water, air conditioning and other aspects of the environment it may be possible to get the hostage-taker to release hostages in exchange for turning utilities back on. The lack of water, for example, in a longer incident might influence 'clean freak' hostage-takers to end the incident.

8 **Use the hostage-taker's own rhetoric against him.** Many terrorist groups claim to be representing the downtrodden or common man; therefore, should they not release those hostages who are 'workers'? This is a chance to appeal to humanitarianism as well.

9 **Avoid negative responses.** Instead of saying 'no' the negotiator should delay or explain that he has to refer the query to a higher authority.

10 **Be positive.** The negotiator must convey the attitude that everything can be worked out, even if he has informed the liaison with the entry team that it appears an entry will be needed.

11 **Downplay the hostages as pawns.** Although the safety of the hostages is of paramount importance to those attempting to resolve a hostage incident, it can be counterproductive to give the hostage-taker the impression that the safety of the hostages is so important that the authorities are impotent.

12 **Keep a record of deadlines and other key events during the negotiations.**

13 **Set up situations in which hostage-takers and hostages have to cooperate.** If the negotiator can encourage such cooperation it builds a bond between the hostage-takers and hostages thus making it harder for the hostage-takers to harm them. One ploy which has been used is to provide food or drink in bulk so that cooperation is necessary to prepare and serve it.

EMOTIONAL INVOLVEMENT

The 'Stockholm Syndrome'

This last technique attempts to use a phenomenon often noted in hostage incidents to the advantage of the hostages. Often called the 'Stockholm Syndrome', this bond between hostage-taker and hostage is normally cited in reference to cases in which the hostages, through dependence on the hostage-takers for their safety, begin to identify with them.

EXAMPLE

The syndrome takes its name from an incident in the summer of 1973. There was a bank robbery in Stockholm which resulted in the taking of hostages. One of the hostages became so involved with her hostage-taker that she later married him. This may be compared to the relationship of some battered women with their abusive husbands. As a result of this syndrome, hostages may actively try to protect the hostage-takers, warning them of the approach of a rescue team or interposing themselves between the hostage-taker and the entry team. In one case, during the rescue at Princes Gate, the youngest terrorist was shielded by women hostages to protect him from the SAS.

The possibility of the Stockholm Syndrome having converted one or more hostages to accomplices is the reason that freed hostages are often restrained and isolated until authorities can ascertain that they are not dangerous. In longer sieges, the hostages may also come to view the authorities as the enemy since they have done nothing to alleviate their distress. FBI behavioural unit studies have even shown that during entries, hostages may be more likely to obey the commands of the hostage-taker than the authorities carrying out the rescue.

On the positive side of the 'Stockholm Syndrome', it may also work to protect the hostages as many hostage-takers have developed a relationship with the hostages which keeps them from killing them. As a result, the negotiator and sniper/observer teams as well as those gathering electronic intelligence should watch for one hostage being removed from the others and maybe even being hooded, as this is often indicative that this hostage is being de-humanised and prepared for execution. Interesting studies have also been done on which hostages are most likely to be chosen as the ones to be made examples of. In various training simulations, the hostage who acted as a sycophant and tried to ingratiate himself with the hostage-takers was chosen because he or she was annoying.

EXAMPLE

At the Princes Gate siege, the hostage who argued in favour of the Ayatollah Khomeini and emphasised flaws in the doctrine espoused by the terrorists was chosen. In still another situation in which hostage-takers and hostages had to sleep in close quarters, the hostage who snored loudly was executed since he had kept everyone awake!

The Negotiator and the 'Stockholm Syndrome'

The hostage negotiator must remember that he, too, can fall prey to the Stockholm Syndrome and must constantly be aware that he does not become overly emotionally involved with the terrorist or hostage-taker on the other end of the telephone. A negotiator who became so wrapped up with talking a terrorist out that he gave even an unintentional warning – 'It's really, really important that you come out right now!' – could prove disastrous if it compromised an entry in progress. It should be noted, however, that though this is a consideration, it is virtually unknown for a negotiator to give away an entry; while again and again negotiators have aided an entry by providing timely intelligence, identifying the most dangerous hostage-taker, or helping to provide a distraction. To put a buffer between the negotiator and those who make the decision about the use of force, an axiom in most hostage rescue units is: negotiators never command and commanders never negotiate.

PSYCHIATRIC ASSESSMENT

The good negotiator will normally have some training in psychology and will employ that training to evaluate the psychological condition of the hostage-takers. Many teams are organised to include a primary negotiator, one or more assistant negotiators to relieve the primary negotiator in lengthy incidents, an intelligence officer to coordinate intelligence gleaned by the negotiator with other intelligence, and a psychologist. Some teams also include a liaison to the SWAT team which will carry out an entry if needed. Although the psychologist will give professional advice on the hostage-taker's state of mind, the negotiator must also be able to draw conclusions and pass significant data on to the psychologist. It is especially important that the negotiator be able to evaluate whether a bond is developing between the hostage-taker and the hostages or if there are indicators the hostage-taker may be reaching the point of violent action.

Many negotiating teams develop worksheets to aid in developing a psychological profile of hostage-takers (see Appendix 3).

The negotiator must be able to use psychological assessment techniques to assess the hostage-

taker's emotional stability at any given point in the incident and be able to judge if the time has come when it is necessary to 'go tactical'. He must also be able to watch the hostage-taker for suicide indicators, because, especially when family members are held hostage, the hostage-taker might take the lives of the hostages, then his own.

Hostage-takers are often categorised into four primary types:

- **Paranoid Schizophrenics:** who will often display delusions of persecution; the negotiator helps this type vent his or her feelings.

- **Psychotic Depressive:** who seems to feel helpless, inadequate and suicide-prone.

- **Anti-Social Personality:** who is selfish and irresponsible; a typical criminal type with a low tolerance for frustration; tends to blame others--a very hard type with whom to negotiate. The best negotiation technique is for the negotiator to convince him that he will help the hostage-taker survive.

- **Inadequate Personality:** who does not respond effectively to situations, a joiner.

Although terrorist hostage-takers may fall into one of these psychological categories, there are certain personality traits which are very common among terrorists. These include low self-esteem and a tendency towards risk taking. Many terrorists externalise and blame outside forces for controlling their lives, thus they often direct hostility towards the forces of social order. The essentially group aspects of terrorism also appeal to many who join terrorist groups – or cults for that matter – because they are looking for place where they can belong.

AUTHOR'S NOTE

In studies of Basque and IRA terrorists, it has been concluded, too, that 'half-breeds' who have one parent who is not Basque or Irish Catholic are more likely to become extremely militant members of the group in an attempt to prove themselves.

PERSONNEL AND TRAINING

SELECTING NEGOTIATORS

In selecting negotiators, it is very useful to have an array of personnel available. For example, it is useful in a multi-racial community to have negotiators of the major races and to be aware when it is important to select a negotiator by race. Some large urban US city hostage rescue teams have found, for example, that it is often not advisable to use a black, female negotiator with a black, male hostage-taker. Obviously, a barricaded white supremacist might not deal well with a black negotiator, while a barricaded black supremacist would not deal well with a white one. In some communities where there are bad feelings between blacks and Hispanics, a white negotiator is viewed as more neutral and may be desirable in some incidents. Having negotiators who are polyglot is an advantage, but linguists should be available who can translate more esoteric languages.

EXAMPLE

In St. Louis where the author lives, for example, a large number of Bosnian refugees have settled so law enforcement agencies need access to reliable Serbo-Croat speakers. A few years ago, the St. Louis FBI office had an agent of Arab extraction who was frequently in demand as a trained law enforcement agent who also spoke Arabic.

JOINT TRAINING

To allow the negotiator to work most effectively with the SWAT team, joint training should be carried out as often as possible. In training scenarios, one useful technique is for the negotiator to role-play a hostage. This allows the negotiator to apply his experience to creating a realistic 'terrorist' but also allows him to get inside the head of his normal 'opponent'. The US Dept of Energy often employs acting students to role-play hostage-takers in scenarios, thus bringing in outsiders who can create more realism for the negotiator and the SWAT team.

No matter how much realism is added to scenarios, however, it may be difficult to create some of the bizarre situations which actually arise.

EXAMPLE

In St. Louis, for example, the police had to respond to an incident in which a trained negotiator and SWAT team commander had taken a police commissioner hostage. Not only did this former officer know the techniques of negotiation, he had actually trained the negotiator with whom he was speaking and had trained the team members who would make an entry. As he spoke with the negotiator he told them exactly what was going on in the CP and with the entry team. This incident, which formed the basis for the film The Negotiator, was solved when the negotiator astutely played upon the unwillingness of the hostage-taker to harm his former team-mates.

EXAMPLE

In another true incident, a jewellery store robbery went wrong, leaving one of the robbers – who was blind! – holding a hostage. Due to the very sensitive hearing of the hostage-taker he picked up anything said in the background around the negotiator and could also hear movement by entry personnel outside the store. The negotiator did, however, calm the hostage-taker and 'negotiate him out'.

Joint training between negotiators and SWAT teams allows each to understand the other's needs and capabilities and avoids the adversarial relationship which has been known to develop if either operates in a vacuum. Negotiators also learn what type of intelligence is critical to the entry team and can often supply timely and relevant data. If allowed to speak with a hostage to 'ascertain that he is all right', a skilful negotiator may gain useful intelligence by asking questions answerable by 'yes' or 'no' (i.e., 'Are all of the hostages held in the same room?' or 'Did you see any explosives?'). Negotiators and SWAT teams often see 'hooks', things asked for by the hostage-taker in different ways. The negotiator sees the hook as a way to get something from the hostage-taker, while the entry team sees the hook as a possible distraction during entry. In many instances, the negotiator can act as a distraction if an entry proves necessary. Just by ringing the phone, he or she can pull a hostage-taker to a given point in a room.

EXAMPLE

A classic example occurred at Princes Gate when the negotiator from the Metropolitan Police kept the terrorist leader on the phone, telling him, as the SAS entered and shot him, 'There is no suspicious movement.'

The good negotiator is absolutely essential in dealing with virtually any hostage incident. He or she may be able to diffuse the situation and talk the hostage-takers out without violence – the most desirable solution. If, however, it proves impossible to negotiate the hostage-taker out, then the negotiator can help provide intelligence for the entry team, can prolong the incident to lull the hostage-takers and allow an effective entry plan to evolve, and may even be able to contribute to the entry by providing a distraction.

Although the men in the black hoods with the submachine guns who do the actual entries are often those portrayed as heroes in the press, it is important to remember that in dozens of hostage incidents around the world in which entries have proved necessary, more hostages died from police gunfire than from terrorist gunfire! Bear in mind, though, that in many of those incidents had the entry not been carried out, even more hostages would have died. Still, the best chance for hostage survival normally rests with the hostage negotiator.

SNIPERS

Although the term 'sniper' is often used generically to describe any marksman who offers the option of long-range engagement and elimination of a threat, there are those who do not consider this the proper term for the police long-range shooter engaged in police hostage rescue operations.

Other terms which are sometimes preferred are 'tactical marksman' or 'sharpshooter' to differentiate the fact that the military sniper's mission, unless assigned to a unit such as Delta Force or the SAS with a hostage rescue mission, is much broader than that of the police tactical marksman.

The police sharpshooter will normally only take a killing shot to save a life, while the military sniper will take shots to eliminate enemy soldiers or disrupt enemy communications or the chain of command.

Having made this distinction, in this chapter the terms 'tactical marksman', 'sharpshooter' and 'sniper' will be used interchangeably.

ROLE OF THE SNIPER

The sniper has myriad responsibilities at a hostage site. He provides intelligence, covers the movement of other personnel, protects innocent bystanders, prevents the escape of a dangerous hostage-taker and eliminates a threat with a precisely placed shot when so ordered. The sniper may also be called upon to create a diversion with gunfire for an entry team. This may entail firing on the side of a building away from the assault. The sniper may also be tasked with shooting out lights which might give away a stealth approach or eliminating vicious attack dogs which endanger the entry team. During the approach of an entry team, the sniper covers them in case they are spotted by one of the hostage-takers. The sniper also protects firefighters, emergency medical technicians, or personnel who might have to move near the site. The sniper helps direct the entry team during an assault, warning them of booby traps, hidden suspects or other dangers. In some cases suspects hidden from the entry team, who may be an immediate threat to that team, may be eliminated by the sniper. Normally, if snipers have to engage multiple hostage-takers, they will have established a priority. In general, the individual with the most dangerous weapon will be eliminated first (i.e., a subject with a submachine gun will be targeted before one with a pistol). Next, subjects considered the most dangerous because of their prior record of violence will be engaged. Finally, those subjects who pose a danger because of their location, either because they are closest to the hostages or are in a position to threaten an entry team, will be engaged.

SELECTION AND TRAINING

When selecting snipers, stress should be put on physical conditioning as the sniper may have to do a substantial amount of climbing to reach his shooting/observation position. Patience is also a critical element in the sniper's make-up since he will often have to wait in position for many hours, yet must still be able to take a precision 'cold' shot if the opportunity presents itself. Many teams prefer to select snipers who have military experience and/or who are hunters as these backgrounds are more likely to provide a precision sniper who will not hesitate to pull the trigger and take the life of a terrorist on command.

Sniper training should incorporate the following skills:

- ammunition choice;

- placement of shots on the target, including placement for an instantaneous kill of the subject;

- sniper-initiated assaults;

- estimation of the effects of wind;

- infiltration to a site;

- camouflage;

- use of optics for range estimation (the Mil Dot, for example - see Diagram 4.1 later in this chapter);

- ballistics (bullet drop);

- sniper deployment;

- coordinated fire;

- shooting through intermediate barriers;

- shooting from different positions;

- rapid target acquisition and shooting;

- target identification;

- shooting at moving targets;

- when to take a shot.

It is very important to incorporate observation exercises for snipers which allow time to view an area, perhaps through binoculars or the rifle scope, then require the sniper to write down what he has seen. Such exercises are invaluable in enhancing the sniper's ability to observe and communicate useful intelligence about the site and hostage-takers to the command post.

DEPLOYMENT

SWAT snipers are normally deployed in two-man sniper/observer teams.

The observer's mission is to:

- observe the site;

- handle communications;

- relieve the sniper on long incidents;

- defend and provide security for the sniper's position;

- call shots for the sniper.

Because of the security function of the observer, many units equip him with an assault rifle equipped with good optics (i.e., the AR-15 or M-16 with an Elcan scope). This allows the observer to provide close range intensive defensive fire, yet still retain a long-range capability. In many units, the observer will also have responsibility for keeping a log of the incident as it relates to the sniper/observer team. This log may be entered as evidence, particularly if the sniper is required to shoot a subject.

THE SNIPER'S BRIEF

Prior to deploying, the sniper/ observer team should be thoroughly briefed on the incident. This will allow them to perform their mission more effectively and also give them a better basis for gathering intelligence. As intelligence is gathered, it is important that the sniper and observer understand the importance of immediately communicating it to the command post or, if an entry is in progress, to the entry team. Some teams deploy the observer with a camera bearing a telephoto lens. Shots of suspects, hostages, a site's interior, etc., may then be taken and used for intelligence and briefing. If such a camera is used, however, arrangements will have to be made to get the film developed and to the CP as soon as possible.

When photos are not available, snipers/observers will often identify subjects by notable physical characteristics for the purpose of communication (i.e., 'Mr Tall' for a very tall subject or 'Miss Redhead'). Communication with other sniper/observer teams is rigorously practiced in modern HR situations, making the threat of crossfire increasingly unlikely. If possible a minimum of four teams is best as this allows the snipers to quarter an area and cover all sides of a site. On the other hand, current standard operating procedure (SOP) with many counterterrorist units is to assign two snipers to each hostage-taker to increase the odds of an instantaneous kill. The decision on how to deploy will be determined by the site and the number of hostage-takers.

THE STALK

While moving into position, the sniper and observer will need to recce the route and cover each other during the stalk. Prior to attempting to move to a hide, the sniper and observer should carry out a 'jump test' to make sure their equipment will not give them away by clanking or rattling. If it is

46

necessary to move down a street when getting into position, it is advisable to move along the left side so that if it is necessary to take cover rapidly in a doorway or alley the rifle may be quickly brought to the right shoulder to deliver fire. It is a sound technique as well to set a variable power sniper scope on the 3X setting while moving, as this allows faster target acquisition with less 'wobble' should a target of opportunity appear. While moving and once in position, the sniper/observer must watch carefully for target indicators such as shine, movement, sound, shape or contrast which will locate potential targets, especially terrorist sentries on a site roof, etc.. In other cases, the sniper and observer may use deception when getting into position. They might, for example, dress as delivery personnel and carry their rifles in long flower boxes so that they could enter a building near the site openly.

CHOOSING THE HIDE

When choosing their hide, the sniper/observer team will try to get as close to the target as possible, in urban areas preferably within 100-200 yards. It is important that command personnel do not try to dictate to the sniper where he should locate his hide. Instead, they must rely on his training and experience and let him choose the position which gives him the best chance of accomplishing his mission. However, even the most competent snipers are well aware that strategies do not always evolve as expected, and will have formed a contingency plan. Many snipers will, in fact, choose their position as well as one or two alternate positions should they need to move after a shot or should the subject spot them and ask the negotiator to remove them. Often, the negotiator will ask for some concession in return for removing the snipers, who will then remove themselves to another hide.

The position chosen should allow observation for intelligence gathering as well as a stable shooting position. When setting up the position, it is important that the sniper/observer be able to view as much of the site as possible, including as many doors and windows as feasible. The position must let them blend into their surroundings and prevent them from being compromised by other people who might stumble on to their position. In evaluating the site as a shooting position, consideration must be given, too, to the possibility of innocent civilians in the background of the shot.

Rooftop Hides

Although in films, it is quite 'visual' to deploy snipers on rooftops and, in reality, sometimes the use of rooftops is necessary, there are many disadvantages to the rooftop hide. Not only might the sniper or observer be silhouetted against the sky, thus revealing his position, but he is also highly visible to press helicopters. Rooftops expose the sniper to the weather as well, eroding his ability to remain in position in heat, cold, rain or snow. In most cases, a rooftop position will require the sniper to fire at a downward angle, while for the best likelihood of success in exact shot placement, the sniper should be roughly on the same level as the target. Being on the same level is particularly critical if a shot might have to be taken through glass. If a rooftop position is absolutely necessary, many teams will deploy with a large cardboard appliance box which may be spray painted to resemble the air conditioning or heating ducts on the rooftop. This box may then serve as a hide on the exposed rooftop.

Gas

Although the sniper/observer wants to get as close as possible, when choosing their position they should give consideration to the possibility that gas will be deployed. If it is, is it likely to reach them? And do they therefore need to deploy with gas masks?

Tips on the Best Urban Hides

The best urban hide will often be in an office or apartment across from the site of the hostage incident. In such a hide, the sniper should open other windows on the same side so the sniping position does not stand out as the only room with an open window. The shooting position should be well back in the room so the rifle's muzzle is not visible. In fact, it is even better if it is slightly offset from the window. Furniture may be moved to establish a stable shooting position. Many snipers carry strips of burlap which may be tacked up in the room to help hide their position from outside as well. It is also advisable to spread a damp cloth under the muzzle to prevent dust being blown up to obscure the rifle's optics after a shot.

MAINTAINING SECURITY

Once established in a position, the sniper/observer must bear in mind that the same things which can locate a subject for them, can give them away. They must, therefore, be careful not to give themselves away through light, noise, movement, shine, reflection or colour. For operations in less urban areas, the sniper must be able to use local flora for camouflage and when building a hide. Many snipers will have a ghillie suit designed to help them blend into the local undergrowth. The rifle will also be camouflaged to blend with the terrain. Wherever the hide is located, the sniper and observer must plan to be in position for an extended period. This means that in addition to their other equipment they should carry food, water and either a plastic bottle or a plastic bag containing a sponge to give them a place to urinate.

AUTHORITY TO SHOOT

Once in position, the sniper/observer will begin to gather and transmit intelligence but must also be prepared to take a shot if necessary.

Many teams use a colour-coded system to give the sniper his authority to shoot a hostage-taker.

- **Green** normally means a shot may be taken as soon as a target is acquired. If the hostage-taker has already killed one or more hostages or there are other indications he is extremely dangerous, the snipers will quite probably have a 'green light'.

- The **yellow** command means that the sniper may only shoot in defence of a life. Thus, if the sniper sees that a hostage-taker is getting ready to execute a hostage or take a shot at a member of the perimeter team he would have the authority to shoot, but not otherwise.

- A **red** light indicates that a shot is not to be taken under any circumstances.

DELIVERING A SHOT

In most situations where a hostage has not yet been killed or injured, the sniper will have a 'yellow light' once in position. The condition of engagement and the time the command is given should be logged by the observer. Snipers train extensively to deliver a shot which will instantly incapacitate a hostage-taker before he can pull a trigger. This necessitates precise shot placement in a very small area. From the front, the shot is normally taken into a triangle formed by the eyes and nose.

If shooting from the rear, the point of aim is just above the shoulder blades at the brain stem. From the side, the sniper aims at the ear canal. Though many other shots from a high-powered rifle would probably result in the death of a subject, the sniper must be skilful enough to secure an 'instant kill'.

SNIPER-INITIATED ENTRY

The sniper will often have the mission of firing to launch a sniper-initiated entry. Such an entry relies on the sniper to eliminate one of the hostage-takers just prior to the entry team assaulting the site. The subject eliminated may be a sentry covering a point of entry, a subject in position to eliminate the hostages, or the leader in order to cause hesitation among the hostage-takers. A countdown may be used during a sniper-initiated entry or in situations where two snipers will fire at a subject simultaneously (i.e., to ensure a quick kill or when firing through glass so that the second shot will come after the glass is already taken out). On a sniper-initiated entry, the countdown might call for the snipers to fire on three, stun grenades or explosive entry devices to be deployed on two and the entry to take place on one. When using two snipers on one target behind a window, some teams have the first sniper fire on two and the second on one. It is also wise to have each sniper give a 'Ready' response earlier in the countdown (i.e., at 10, 9, or 8) to make sure that everyone is prepared. Many teams also give the 'fire' command twice to ensure that it is clear. In fact, the policy in these teams is that the shot will only be taken if the sniper hears, 'Fire! Fire!' This allows for the possibility of a break in communication whereby the sniper would only hear, 'Fire' when the actual transmission might be, 'The suspect is coming out. Do not fire.'

OVERCOMING BARRIERS

As has already been mentioned, snipers need to be aware of the problems presented by intermediate barriers between them and the target, particularly windows, fencing and screens.

Windows
When firing through windows, there are five basic rules:

1 Use a rifle of .308 calibre or greater as the heavier bullet will be more resistant to deflection.

2 Try to fire at as close to a 90 degree angle as possible.

3 Use two shooters whenever possible.

4 Try to shoot when the subject is close to the glass so that deflection will be less magnified.

5 Take a shot at the largest possible area (i.e., body rather than head) so a small amount of deflection won't be as critical.

If the hostage-taker is in a car, he will normally be relatively close to the glass, but the 'starring' of safety glass, which does not shatter, may make it difficult to see for a second shot. If the hostage-taker is in a school bus, passenger bus or train, he may be much further from the glass, thus increasing the possibility of deflection. When taking a shot through non-safety glass, the sniper must be aware of the potential 'spalling' effect, which can hurl shards of glass towards hostages as well as hostage-takers within the room. Generally, however, if a sniper is called upon to fire, the hostages will be in more imminent danger from the hostage-taker and the chance of cuts becomes a calculated risk.

Fencing

When firing through chain-link fencing, the sniper should get the muzzle as close to the fencing as possible to lower the possibility of deflection; of course, if the hostage-taker is directly behind a fence this is not really possible. This may be a situation where having one sniper on the same level with the target and a second located to shoot down and over the fence would be tactically sound. Another tactic is to avoid a shot through chain-link fence. If such a shot must be taken from the same level as the target, then, as with glass, multiple snipers should be used

and they should fire at a 90 degree angle; fire when the subject is as close to the fence as possible and aim for the largest possible target area.

Windscreens

When firing through windscreens, accuracy is normally not adversely affected at ranges of 100 yards or less; however; it may be easier to see through the screen if the sniper is located at a 90 degree angle to the target.

RANGE ESTIMATION

LOW-LIGHT CONDITIONS

Hostage incidents may play out in such a way that an entry will take place at night or the sniper may be required to take a shot at night. Lack of light substantially increases the difficulty of taking a precise shot; however, the skilled tactical marksman will have practised shots in low light conditions and will have learned certain specialised techniques which will make him more effective in low light. By learning to keep his eyes active and scanning at night he will be more likely to identify a target.

By looking a few degrees to the left of a potential target, he will also find that it will actually be clearer at night. The sniper must also remember that at night it is easy to overestimate range to a light source. By training at night with illuminated targets at varying ranges, he can become more adept at range estimation. A scope with an illuminated reticle can also help substantially if it is necessary to take a shot at night.

AUTHOR'S NOTE

Sniping expert John Plaster suggests in his work *The Ultimate Sniper* that for night sniping, it may be desirable to have either the observer or both the sniper and observer armed with an M-16 which has highly effective night vision optics.

Finally, to protect his night vision, the sniper should use a red-filtered flashlight if he needs a light source.

Although range estimation is difficult at night, there are techniques which make it much easier during daylight.

For example, in US urban situations, city blocks are often of a standard length. Likewise, two-lane or four-lane highways may be of standard width. By being aware of these standard distances, range estimation will be much easier. Compact commercial laser range designators, which may be very useful in estimating range, are also available.

'RULE OF THUMB' METHOD

Some snipers also use a literal 'rule of thumb' estimation method. By extending the arm and placing the thumb in the 'thumbs up' position, the sniper may then place the edge of the thumbnail directly under the target. By counting the number of paces it would theoretically take the individual to walk to the other edge of the thumbnail, range can roughly be estimated by allowing 50 yards for each pace. Thus, if it would take the subject two paces to cross the nail, the range is approximately 100 yards.

THE MIL DOT SYSTEM

Most tactical rifle scopes incorporate some aid to range estimation as well.

The Mil Dot system which is widely used by military and police snipers is a good example.

AUTHOR'S NOTE

Originally developed for the USMC, a recent informal survey by two of the foremost sniper trainers in the US suggested that one third to one half of trainees are taught the technique. Snipers will, of course, also learn the technicalities of laser ranging systems and other more complex methods of estimating range. However, the Mil Dot remains an established tactic, whose wide use is perhaps partially due to the fact that it does not depend on additional equipment, such as batteries, to enable it to function.

The Mil Dot reticle employs wide posts which lead the eye to a series of dots leading from each post to the centre of the reticle. Each dot is a milliradian (mil) apart if measured centre to centre from the cross hairs. At 100 yards a mil equals 3.6 inches and at 1000 yards equals 36 inches or one yard. By learning a simple formula: (height of target in yards) X 1000 / height of target in mils = range in yards. For example, if a sniper is observing the hostage-taker and has the target's head in his cross hairs, he may assume that the head is approximately nine inches high or 1/4 yard. If the head covers two mils in the reticle, the distance may be determined by the following calculation: 1/4 x 1000 = 250 / 2 resulting in a range calculation of 125 yards to the hostage-taker's head. With practice

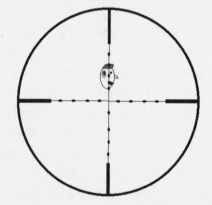

4.1 USING THE DOT RANGE DETERMINATION SYSTEM

Explanation: Note that the head of the hostage-taker fits centre-to-centre between two Mil Dots. The normal head-crown-to-chin measures about 9 inches. Therefore, the range is calculated as follows: Height of Target in Yards (1/4) x 1000 / Height of Target in Mils (2) Thus, 250/2 = a range of 125 yards.

this calculation may be carried out very quickly (see Diagram 4.1).

Once the range is estimated, the sniper must allow for the drop or trajectory of the bullet. To do this effectively, he needs range tables for the load he is using which quickly tell him how many clicks (usually in one-quarter minute of angel (MOA), or 1/4 inch increments) he will need to adjust the scope. Thus, if the drop of the bullet at a certain range is nine inches, the sniper will adjust the scope's elevation by nine full MOA clicks.

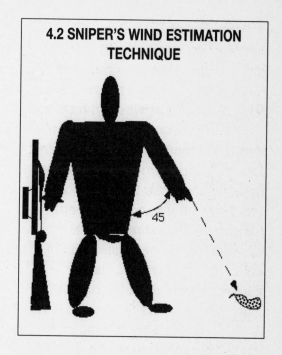

4.2 SNIPER'S WIND ESTIMATION TECHNIQUE

45

ADJUSTING FOR WINDAGE

Not only must a good sniper be able to estimate the distance to the target, but he must be able to estimate if there is a cross wind which will affect the bullet's flight. To give an illustration of how important adjusting for windage can be, at 300 yards, a 10mph cross wind can affect the impact of a 168 grain .308 bullet by seven to eight inches, enough to make the difference between an incident-ending head shot and a miss! To estimate cross winds, experienced snipers have certain tricks. One is based on observing his surroundings. If the wind is just barely felt against the face, it is blowing at 3-5mph; if it causes consistent movement of leaves on the trees, it is blowing at 5-8mph; if leaves or loose paper blows across the ground, it is blowing at 8-12mph; and if small trees are swaying, it is blowing at 12-15mph.

Another method employs rudimentary geometry. The sniper drops a small piece of paper or a piece of grass and watches its fall. He then points at where it hit the ground. By taking the angle of the arm to the body and dividing it by four, the approximate windage may be estimated (see Diagram 4.2). Wind can be a special problem for snipers operating in urban environments where buildings of different heights may cause air currents which affect the bullet's flight. Most snipers have some way of quickly accessing ballistic data in the field to allow scope adjustments for windage and elevation. Some use small laminated cards attached to the rifle's stock, while others use a small device known as the 'Pathfinder' which fits on to the scope and allows a tape with ballistic data to be quickly pulled out and viewed. Small computers are also currently available into which ballistic data may be punched to arrive at proper adjustments for a particular situation.

It should be apparent that not only must a good sniper be patient, an excellent stalker and a superb marksman, but he must also be a skilled field physicist.

THE SNIPER'S KIT

To deal with the wind and longer ranges, some counterterrorist snipers are equipped with rifles more powerful than the standard .308. Many choose the .300 Winchester Magnum round, which, using the 200 grain Federal Boat Tail Soft Point (BTSP), has an outstanding ballistic coefficient and a flat trajectory. Also popular with some units is the .338 Lapua round. Units such as the SAS, Delta Force and SEAL Team Six even have sniping rifles chambered for the .50 Browning MG round, which allow engagement of targets out to a mile. Though those weapons are primarily designed for use against material such as radar sites or communications centres, in the hands of skilled users, precision .50 sniping rifles can reach out and hit a hostage-taker at 1,000 yards or more.

Whatever rifle is chosen – and overwhelmingly it will be one of the high quality .308 models – each sniper should be issued his own rifle so that he will be familiar with its foibles and its trigger pull. The precision sniping rifle must also be carried in a case designed to protect the rifle and its optics. The sniper may well have to fire a 'cold' shot under great pressure without a chance to test his scope's alignment on site. As a result, protecting the sniping rifle from punishment which can affect the optics is absolutely critical. Eagle Industries offers a useful product in their sniper pad, which is a well padded case for the sniping rifle, which when folded out makes a pad on which the sniper may lay for prone shots. Some snipers carry their rifles in a hard case for even greater protection.

The sniper has immense responsibility during a hostage incident. Not only must he provide timely and critical intelligence to other members of the hostage rescue team, but he may have the opportunity to end the incident and save lives with one well-placed shot. Although hostage rescue units would prefer to end an incident with no loss of life, if it is necessary for a hostage-taker to die in order to save the lives of hostages or personnel who would carry out the assault, then the sniper has the best chance of ending the incident surgically. The sniper must also be willing even under pressure to say no to a shot, to admit that he is not confident that he can make the shot under the circumstances then in place.

The snipers on the best hostage rescue teams go through rigorous selection and training and are justly respected by the other members of the team for their unique skills. But they, and their unit commander, must remember that all of that training may well have to be focused on one second in time, one breath, one trigger pull!

CHAPTER 5

ENTRY AND CLEARING TECHNIQUES IN HOSTAGE AND BARRICADE SITUATIONS

Although incidents involving barricaded subjects have many of the same characteristics as the hostage situation and, in fact, many agencies use the term 'barricaded suspect' to include cases where the suspect is inside a building or another site with a hostage, for purposes of this discussion, a 'barricaded suspect' will refer to an armed terrorist, criminal, or mentally disturbed person who has taken up a position where he presents a danger to himself or others.

EXAMPLE

Among the most dangerous of barricaded subjects are those such as the 'Texas Tower' sniper during the 1960s who climbed to a position on top of a building on the University of Texas campus and began killing people at random. The controversial standoff and raid at the Branch Davidian compound in Waco, Texas, may also be viewed as a type of barricade situation, though the FBI eventually used the rationale that children in the compound were, in effect, hostages when they moved against the Branch Davidians (see Appendix 1). Barricade situations may also occur after a subject has already murdered or injured someone.

DEFINING THE BARRICADE SITUATION

Whether it is a suspect who has killed a law enforcement officer, then fled to a residence or other building, or a distraught husband who has killed his estranged wife then refused to surrender to authorities, many of the elements remain the same: an armed subject who has proved a willingness to take a life ensconced in a building and unwilling to surrender. Perhaps the type of barricade situation the authorities fear most is one in which a group of terrorists have occupied some critical installation – a nuclear power plant or a biological warfare research centre, for example. Or a barricade situation might arise in which terrorists have occupied a national monument or symbol and placed explosives – at the Washington Monument or Eiffel Tower, for example.

'NEGOTIATING OUT' THE BARRICADED SUBJECT

In the most common barricade situations, the hostage negotiator will attempt to convince the suspect to surrender, much as in a hostage situation, though the removal of the hostage element also removes a certain element of pressure from the negotiator. On the other hand, in barricade situations, the negotiator will have to work at lowering the perception of the authorities as a threat. This may be accomplished by using a lower profile containment than with a hostage situation where it is important to send the message that there is the capability to exert force if a hostage is harmed. The negotiator will also want to demonstrate patience, perhaps even keep talking if the subject refuses to answer. He will also attempt to provide nonviolent resolution options to the barricaded subject.

EXAMPLE

Some of the negotiators involved in the Branch-Davidian siege at Waco felt that the FBI HRT took many actions which exacerbated the situation rather than defused it. In part, this arose because some viewed the incident as a hostage situation because of children in the compound who were allegedly being sexually abused, while others viewed it as a barricade situation.

Some barricade situations may well result, in fact, from hostage situations once the hostages have been released, yet the hostage-taker refuses to surrender. In these situations, the negotiator focuses on ending the siege without the loss of the subject's life or the lives of any of the containment or entry personnel. Without the presence of hostages, it is quite likely that snipers will not have a green light to shoot unless the subject has access to explosives or begins shooting at officers or bystanders.

EXAMPLE

One case of this type involved a 'barricaded' suspect who had climbed to a position on a bridge across the Missouri River and begun shooting at cars approaching the bridge. In a situation such as this where a major artery was being interdicted, the snipers might well have been given the green light to eliminate the threat had he not surrendered relatively quickly.

PROTECTING INNOCENTS

Negotiators and other hostage rescue personnel cannot be certain that what seems to be a barricade situation is not actually a hostage situation either. There may be a hostage being held without the authorities being aware of it. In a large building containing an 'active shooter', there may also be innocent residents or workers trapped who, though not hostages in the strictest sense, are still in danger from the shooter, particularly if he begins to move through the building. When planning an entry in what seems to be a barricade situation, SWAT personnel, therefore, have to operate on the assumption that they may encounter innocents as they move through a site. In the UK this practice of 'search to contact' is rarely used in barricade situations, where stand-off negotiation is preferred. However, the possibility of encountering an armed suspect or even 'active shooter' in a US incident demands a more confrontational approach.

'SUICIDE BY COP'

At least some barricade situations will be part of what has come to be known as 'suicide by cop'. Some mentally disturbed persons who precipitate a hostage or barricade situation do so specifically with the hopes that the police will kill them. Although such subjects may have a death wish, they can still be extremely dangerous to police officers and hostages or bystanders as they may threaten or shoot others to force the authorities to take action against them. Normally, the best chance at saving such individuals is through an expert negotiator who can convince the subject that his life does have some value. All reasonable attempts will be made to contain and neutralise a subject attempting to bring about his own death, but should he threaten the lives of SWAT teams or others, he may have to be given his wish. The primary mission of the SWAT team is to make certain that he does not have a chance to take anyone else with him.

If SWAT personnel have a high degree of confidence that there are no innocent bystanders or hostages present in a site containing a barricaded suspect, then methods of clearing the site without endangering personnel may be desirable.

CLEARING A SITE WITHOUT HOSTAGES

K9

Many SWAT teams either incorporate K-9 units or work closely with K-9 units. Without the problem of the dogs being able to differentiate hostage from hostage-taker – though most K-9 dogs are trained to go for the subject with a weapon – sending in trained dogs to clear a building is a viable tactical option. In fact, because SWAT dogs are often used to search buildings for armed suspects, body armour for police or military dogs is now widely used. The SWAT dog will have undergone specialised training which is somewhat different from that of the typical police dog. The SWAT dog, for example, must be able to crawl long distances for insertions into buildings. He must also respond to hand signals as well as verbal signals and be used to flash, bang distraction devices. The SWAT dog will also normally receive more obstacle training and be especially good at tracking by scent. Because he will most likely be dealing with an armed suspect and must give the entry team time to reach him, the SWAT dog is trained to deliver multiple bites aggressively on a suspect (as opposed to the 'bite and hold' approach of normal police dogs). Though their usefulness in hostage rescue is severely limited, the trained SWAT dog can be invaluable in dealing with a barricaded suspect. Unfortunately, because suspects will probably be well-armed, it can be quite dangerous for the SWAT dog.

If the decision is made to use dogs to clear a site, there are various tactical options. Since even the best trained dogs are not capable of opening doors, the most likely scenario is that handlers will insert K-9s into a building to search a specified area (i.e., the entrance foyer). Once the dog returns to indicate no one has been found an entry team can then follow up to double check. The dog will then be inserted into the next area to be cleared. For this tactic to be most effective, the K-9 teams should have trained with the SWAT team and the dogs should be familiar with the SWAT team members and the tactics which will be employed.

TEAR GAS

Another widely used tactic when dealing with barricaded subjects who do not hold hostages is the deployment of chemical agents (tear gas). Normally, these chemical agents will be inserted to contaminate an enclosed space and force the subject out. Chemical agents may be deployed in various forms. The most effective are generally pyrotechnic combustion devices which produce smoke containing the agent. However, these devices usually carry a substantial risk of fire which will destroy the area in which deployed. Some SWAT teams have, however, developed containers for the pyrotechnic devices which allow them to be used with far less chance of fire. Chemical agents may also be deployed by blast dispersion in powder form, in liquid form, as an aerosol liquid, as a fog or as dust from a launched projectile. A widely used method for introducing chemical agents is the 37mm Ferret round fired from a gas gun or a grenade launcher mounted beneath the barrel of an M-16/AR-15 rifle. These rounds, which deliver 16 grams of the agent in liquid form, may be fired directly through glass into an area. To offer a comparison, a pyrotechnic combustion device would normally contain about 75 grams of the agent, almost five times as much as the Ferret.

There are three types of chemical agent (often generically called 'tear gas') which may be used in riot control or barricade situations:

- **CN (Chloroacetophenone).** Normally colour-coded red on the projectile, in small quantities, CN has an odor of apple blossoms. It is very fast acting, affecting the lachrymal glands to cause tearing in one to three seconds. Among its effects are closing of the eyes, heavy tearing, coughing, sneezing, runny nose and itching or burning on the skin. It can also irritate open wounds. CN reactions will normally last for 30-45 minutes.

- **CS (Orthochlorobenzalmalononitrile).** Normally colour-coded blue on the projectile, CS has replaced CN with most SWAT teams. Relatively fast acting, CS affects the respiratory system very quickly and the lachrymal glands within about three to seven seconds. Among its effects are closing of the eyes, stinging and burning on the skin after about ten minutes, runny nose, breathing difficulty and burning lungs.

- **OC (Oleoresin Capsicum).** Although the colour codes for CN and CS are international, OC does not have a standard international colour designation, though its projectiles are normally coloured orange. Its effects include eye closing and burning with direct exposure, coughing and retching, breathing difficulty and burning on direct contact with the skin.

There are many variables which can influence the effects of chemical agents. Some individuals are highly resistant to the effects of the various agents, especially if they are on drugs or alcohol. On the other hand, extended exposure to high levels of the agents can lead to death in some individuals, particularly those with respiratory problems. Formulae are available to units which use gas to allow them to calculate the amount of gas needed to fill a cubic area effectively and the time before it should take effect. Research has also been carried out to determine at what level the potential for exposure proving fatal becomes critical. This data indicates that for CN to be potentially lethal, 175 times the incapacitation dosage must be introduced. For CS 1,250 times the incapacitation dosage must be introduced. Obviously, the margin of safety is substantially greater with CS, one of the reasons it has replaced CN with most SWAT teams.

Gas has proved highly effective in forcing suspects to vacate a site. However, it must be borne in mind that some subjects may take measures to counter the effects of gas, some as simple as lying on the floor, others as sophisticated as using surplus gas masks/respirators. More than one officer has been killed by a subject while attempting to clear a building which has had chemical agents introduced. As a result, entry teams should do substantial training in their gas masks so that they are aware of how much their vision is limited. Shooting scenarios wearing the masks and in smoke/gas filled rooms should also be set up so that personnel can operate more confidently in a gas-filled environment. Perimeter personnel and snipers must also be alert once chemical agents have been introduced as some subjects will choose to come out shooting.

NBC BARRICADE SITUATIONS

Some barricade situations might include Nuclear, Biological or Chemical threats. Thus, they become the ultimate hostage situation since, in effect, an entire city may be held hostage. In the US, the FBI and specialists from the Department of Energy and other agencies will eventually respond to such a crisis; however, it may still fall to SWAT personnel to handle many aspects of an NBC barricade situation.

NBC CONTAINMENT

As a result, counterterrorist/SWAT personnel need to understand containment and confinement procedures for hazardous materials. Often, combined training with firefighters will help develop a joint response. One of the important steps for counterterrorist

personnel who initially respond to this type of situation is to determine how much of a 'down wind' hazard they may be facing so an evacuation order may be given. It may well be necessary, too, when dealing with a possible terrorist incident involving hazardous materials that a far larger perimeter be established than usual.

THE HAZMAT ENVIRONMENT

Some urban SWAT teams, including New York City's Emergency Services Unit, have trained to operate in MOPP (Mission Oriented Protective Posture) Suits. Part of the responsibility of a counterterrorist/SWAT unit when hazardous materials are involved, particularly if they are biological agents, is the prevention of anyone leaving a potentially contaminated area. As a result, teams should practise restraint techniques while wearing the MOPP suits. Most tactical teams have found that for their purposes relatively inexpensive Level A or B disposable suits are a better choice than the very expensive suits designed for use by chemical warfare researchers or specialists from the

Center for Disease Control. It is quite likely, too, that in barricade incidents involving HazMat that SWAT personnel will be primarily concerned with dealing with the human threat of terrorists or deranged persons, while specialists will deal with the actual materials. Some considerations will, however, have to be given to using firearms in the HazMat environment. Submachine guns equipped with 'wet suppressors', which will substantially limit muzzle flash, would be one option. Care must be taken in shooting in any HazMat environment, too, since a stray bullet could rupture a container, thus increasing the possibility of contamination. In cases involving potentially deadly biological agents, no one who has been exposed may be allowed to leave a containment area. As a result, snipers may be given a broad 'green light' to shoot anyone who refuses to stay within a containment area. SWAT teams assigned to sensitive installations such as nuclear power plants will be trained particularly for dealing with an incident in their venue. As a result, they will know

which parts of a site are most sensitive and where the likely points of danger are. Therefore, they will know how to carry out an entry that contains intruders away from the most critical parts of the installation. They will also understand that to prevent a situation which might prove hazardous to hundreds of thousands or millions of people, they may have take very draconian measures to stop intruders.

> More discussion will be given to entries at specialised sites in the next chapter.

ENTRIES

Whether carrying out entries at a hostage or a barricade incident, the basic organisation and tactics of the entry team remain the same. Entry teams are normally organised into four or five man elements. In the UK it is most likely to be four men. **The breakdown of organisation given below is based on five being present** (see Diagrams 5.1 and 5.2).

5.1 FIVE-MAN ENTRY

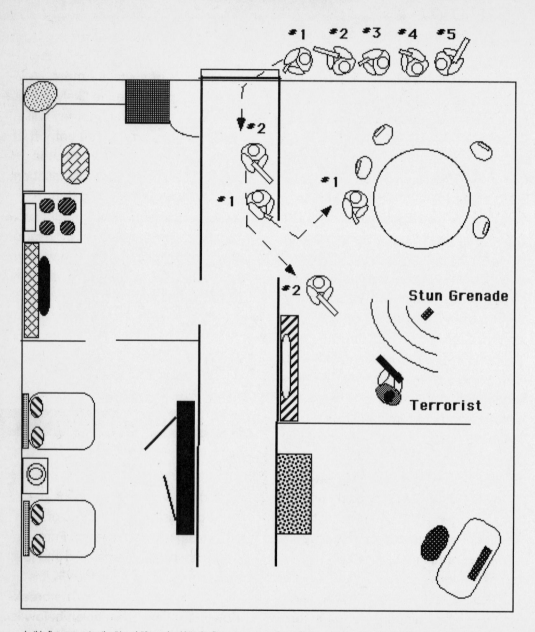

In this five-man entry, the #1 and #2 men lead into the first room using a Cross-Button entry (see 5.5). The following team members will secure the hallway after them. #1, who was first into the room, would have engaged the armed terrorist, with #2, the submachine gunner, giving additional fire if needed.

5.2 FIVE-MAN ENTRY ON A MULTI-ROOM SITE

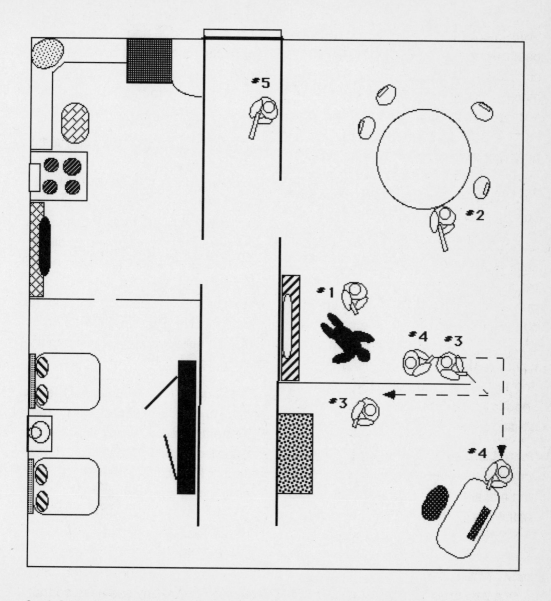

Once the first room is secure, entry men #3 and #4 move through to enter the next room, while #1 and #2 deal with the downed suspect and secure the first room. Entry man #5 provides security by covering the hallway and exits from the rooms.

1 **Point man.** The point man will normally be armed with a handgun so that he can have one hand free for deploying a mirror or SWAT Cam to look around corners, to open doors, or to throw in a stun grenade. The point man is generally designated a 'primary shooter', which means he will engage the first threat encountered when coming through the door.

2 **Clearing Man.** The clearing man, the second man through the door, is frequently armed with a submachine gun and will engage additional targets encountered upon entry. The point man and the number two clearing man must have practised their methods of entry and technique for dividing the room for shooting purposes to avoid a crossfire situation (see Diagram 5.3).

3 **Team Leader.** The team leader may be armed with a handgun or a submachine gun and acts as a secondary shooter to deal with any threats still not eliminated by the first two men through the door. His positioning allows him to make rapid decisions or rapidly change tactics based upon circumstances encountered during the entry. He will

also help subdue and control any suspects encountered during the entry so that the first two men can move on to the doorway to the next room.

4 **Clearing Man.** The fourth man is armed with a shotgun on many teams and has the responsibility for blowing off door locks or hinges with special shotgun munitions. He is also a secondary shooter, though unless his shotgun is specially choked to allow head shots on a hostage-taker, he will normally sling the shotgun and use a handgun if it is necessary to shoot near hostages. He is also a 'take-up' man who will help deal with any suspects encountered.

5 **Rear Guard:** Many teams use the rear guard to deal with doors using a ram or other entry device, which will then be discarded so that he can provide rear security for the entry element or give assistance if it is needed.

If suspects are encountered on entry, follow up teams may either pass through a room secured by the first team or secure any suspects so that the initial team can quickly move on to clear additional rooms. If no suspects are encountered, the initial team will quickly move on to clear additional rooms. Some type of concise yet clear radio drill is important to avoid confusion during these room clearing operations. For example, a point man who has cleared one room and is moving to the next one, might state, 'Clear, Moving!'. Or, if the lead two men have secured the first room but are dealing with suspects, the command for the next men to move into the next room might be, 'Clear, Clear, Go!'. If there are hostages at the site, once an entry begins, the teams, which will often be entering from more than one point, must clear the building as quickly as possible in order to maximise the chances of saving the hostages.

Normally, an entry team will neutralise terrorist/hostage-taker threats in the following order:

1 Immediate danger to the entry team.

2 Immediate danger to the hostages.

3 Attempting to escape.

4 Surrendering.

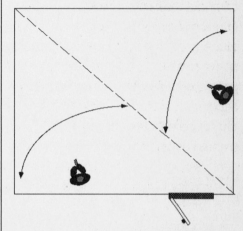

5.3 SAFE ARCS OF FIRE DURING ROOM ENTRIES

During two-man room entries, team members should mentally divide the room in half and limit their arcs of fire to prevent the possibility of hitting their partner. An exception to this rule may arise if one entry man spots an immediate threat within his partner's arc of fire which the man assigned to that area seems to have missed and when he is confident he can take the shot without endangering the partner. An example might be an armed suspect in a closet visible only to the entry man in the opposite half of the room.

However, a member of the entry team may make a conscious decision to deal with an immediate danger to a hostage over immediate danger to himself based on the fact he is wearing body armour or confidence that another member of the team will deal with the threat. The standard logic, though, is that if an officer is hit, he will not be able to carry on with the rescue efforts will normally be made to neutralise threats to the entry team first. Since well-trained team members will carry out their entry quickly, often after pitching in a stun grenade, threats to the team and to the hostages will normally be neutralised virtually simultaneously. As both hostage-takers and hostages are secured by the 'take-up men' they should be checked for weapons, explosives and injuries. In the cases of serious injuries, either follow-up Emergency Medical Technicians (EMTs) or a doctor assigned to the unit will enter the secured area to treat the injured party.

AUTHOR'S NOTE

In units such as the SAS or Delta Force where members of the unit are highly trained field medics, those giving medical assistance will also be armed and capable of defending themselves or the patient if necessary. On at least one major US SWAT Team a doctor, formerly a Special Forces medic, is a full member of the team. All teams plan in advance for the possibility of having to evacuate an injured team member under fire. GSG-9 even inserts and tapes down an IV needle into the arm of each entry team member prior to an assault to speed treatment if he is hit.

If there are any indications that explosives may be present, bomb technicians will also be available to follow-up the entry team once an area or the entire site is secure.

If an entry is deemed necessary, it must be borne in mind that entries have great potential for injury to hostages or rescue personnel. That is why, if possible, it is highly preferable to end a barricade or hostage situation through negotiation or sniper fire, rather than assault.

If an entry is deemed necessary there are two primary types of entry:

- stealth or penetration, and
- dynamic or breach.

STEALTH ENTRY

The stealth entry is designed to allow team members to get as close to the hostage-taker or suspect as possible before he or she knows they are there. As a result, the entry team uses stealthy movement maximising concealment and cover, makes maximum use of the intelligence available to enter at a point not visible to the suspect and remains as quiet as possible, using hand signals for communication and avoiding squeaky steps or other giveaways. Normally, it is best if an entry team moves in the order it will carry out the entry. One important precaution is to take care that no one inadvertently presses the switch for a gun-mounted light or laser, since in some cases pressure switches are used. A SWAT Cam video system, which employs a camera on an extendible pole and a viewing screen, will often be used when moving carefully through a building during the approach. The point man may also employ an inspection mirror on a folding extender for the same purpose. A variation of the stealth or penetration entry is the infiltration of entry team members posing as delivery personnel or maintenance workers. In any stealth or infiltration entry, the team must be prepared to 'go dynamic' at any point when their approach is compromised, particularly if hostages are involved. In many cases, a second entry team is ready to carry out an explosive or breaching

entry should the stealth approach become compromised. If entering from a single location, it is also important to have a second entry point already planned in case a problem arises with the initial point of entry.

DYNAMIC ENTRY

In a dynamic or breach entry, the object is to get into the site as rapidly as possible to shock and confuse subjects before they can react. Speed, though team members should not run, is paramount in the dynamic entry, which frequently results in the use of explosives to open a portal through a wall or to blow a door. Rams, hooligan bars, glass breakers, or shotguns with Shok-Lok rounds to blow off locks or hinges may be a key part of such an entry.

Both stealth and dynamic entries will be covered in greater detail in the following chapter.

DISTRACTION

With either type of entry, distraction may be employed. The negotiator may aid in distracting the barricaded suspect or the hostage-taker by keeping him on the phone talking, as in the SAS operation at Princes Gate, or may actually ring the phone to pull him to a known location just prior to the entry. On a sniper-initiated entry, the sniper may fire at one of the suspects deemed especially dangerous, thus creating confusion through the noise of the shot and the incapacitation of the suspect. The sniper may also shoot out a light or a television to create a diversion. Helicopters are often used to create a diversion and also to cover any sound of movement as an entry team moves into its final position outside of a door or window. Another distraction which has been used frequently is the siren of an approaching ambulance or other emergency vehicle.

EXAMPLE

During the Italian rescue of General Dozier from the Red Brigade, road construction outside the building where he was being held both acted as a distraction and covered the approach of the entry team (see Appendix 1).

The negotiator may also seem to give in to the suspect's demands to lull him and draw his attention to a window as police vehicles begin to pull back and leave. Akin to a distraction is the situation in which the negotiator explains something away which might alert the subject to an impending entry. For example, he might say, 'In a couple of minutes, you might hear what sounds like a chainsaw. One of our men got trapped in a vehicle and we're trying to get him out.' In actuality, the sound would be the entry team cutting through a security door. The type of distraction is limited only by the creativity of the hostage rescue team and by the circumstances of the incident.

BOOBY TRAPS

During the entry, officers must be aware of potential booby traps. Although entry teams encounter booby traps most often when serving high-risk warrants against drug dealers or clandestine drug labs, there is still the possibility that a site may have been booby trapped, particularly if a barricaded suspect has been planning a confrontation with authorities for some time.

Among the types of booby traps which have been encountered are:

- set guns (usually shotguns set to be triggered by a trip wire),

- improvised explosive devices,

- steps removed from stairways,

- trap doors which can drop an officer one or more storeys through a floor,

- fish hooks strung on line at eye level and

- weighted objects above doors.

Because of its slower, more measured movement, an entry team carrying out a stealth or penetration entry is more likely to spot booby traps. If explosive booby traps are encountered during a hostage rescue operation, it may be necessary to note them for other teams which will follow-on, then bypass them until EOD personnel can deal with them.

AUTHOR'S NOTE

At least one team carries bright, reflective, stick-on explosive signs of the type used for trucks to post as a booby trap warning.

The possibility of encountering interior fortifications must also be borne in mind, as hostage-takers and barricaded suspects have been known to move furniture, block doors and otherwise make a room highly difficult to enter.

There are other basic precepts which many entry teams follow, most of which are based on common sense and experience. For example, team members avoid silhouetting themselves in doors or windows. When moving near closed doors, they also remain aware that their shadows may be seen under a door. When the hostage-taker or subject is in a room without doors, experience has shown that it may be better to do an entry through the windows or a simultaneous entry through the doorway and a window. Cupboards can be especially dangerous since many suspects have chosen to hide in them. When clearing a cupboard, entry personnel will usually assign one man to cover the cupboard as the other jerks open the door. When clearing a large building such as an office block or a school, many entry teams use some type of wedge, tie or lock to secure doors of rooms which have been declared secure. When moving, entry teams are aware that unless dealing with a highly trained individual, it normally takes four to five seconds for a subject to acquire a target and shoot. As a result, entry team members try to remain exposed for only three seconds or less when moving between points of concealment or cover. Entry teams are also aware that when doing an entry and clearing a room, it is better to avoid the corners as they will be more susceptible to hostile fire. If doing an entry from multiple points, great care must be taken so that no one falls prey to 'friendly fire'. If entries are carried out on multiple levels of a building, normally a team should not move to a level covered by another team to avoid the danger of engaging fellow members of the hostage rescue unit.

AUTHOR'S NOTE

One aid to avoiding 'friendly fire' is to have each team member dress the same with ID ('FBI', 'POLICE') prominently displayed on their ballistic vests or uniforms. The combination of gas mask and/or balaclava and black uniform may also inspire a certain degree of awe in hostage-takers, thus causing them to hesitate a second or two before initiating action.

THE HIDDEN SUSPECT

Particularly in barricade situations there may be a tendency for the subject to move upwards in a building, often even to hide in the attic. As a result, entry teams when searching a building must be constantly aware of the potential threat from above. If a subject's location in a building is not known and there is little intelligence about his actions or movements, it is best to assume the worst-case scenario.

- Unless absolutely certain he is unarmed, assume he is.
- Assume he is dangerous and will

attempt to kill members of the entry team.

- If his armament is not known, assume he is armed with a high-powered rifle which can punch through ballistic vests and body bunkers.

- If his location is not known, assume that he will be in the worst and most inconvenient location within the site.

DECLARING THE SITE SECURE

Once a site has been cleared, before it is declared fully secure, the unit commander will generally have each team member report in via radio with data about himself or other team members within his sight, hostages and hostage-takers or suspects. He will note anyone needing medical attention and the degree of the injuries. If explosives or booby traps are present in his area he will report that too. A final sweep will probably be carried out, as well, to check potential hiding places more thoroughly before the entry teams stand down.

TRAINING ON ENTRY AND ROOM CLEARING

Hostage rescue teams train on entries and room clearing techniques constantly. In an attempt to make scenarios as realistic as possible some units such as the SAS and the FBI HRT have trained with live hostages and live ammunition. However, to lessen the chance of accidental injury, many of these same units now use sophisticated video equipment which allows the use of live hostages and hostage-takers projected onto a shooting range. Many units also use tyre houses for training to set up live fire exercises. Even more sophisticated training facilities exist which employ a rubberised type of concrete which actually absorbs bullets.

Shooting drills for entry teams should include:

- scenarios involving close-range shooting (i.e., 1-15 yards),

- various types of lighting,
- tight spaces,
- multiple targets,
- a combination of 'shoot' and 'no-shoot' (hostage) targets and
- smoke and noise.

At least a portion of shooting practice should be carried out wearing full tactical gear and gas masks. Training is also carried out using paint guns, Simunitions (paint-filled bullets), or laser weapons which allow realistic engagement of targets which 'shoot back'. Teams often train in venues such as schools, courthouses and office buildings where they might have to carry out an actual rescue.

THE BALLISTIC SHIELD

During their training, entry teams rehearse certain basic room entry and clearing manoeuvres until they become extremely fast and skilful. Many teams equip the point man with a 'body bunker' or ballistic shield to gain additional protection against a surprise shot when carrying out the initial move into a building or up stairways. In the latter case, especially, however, it is important to remember when using a ballistic shield that an officer is vulnerable to a shot from above. A Level IV shield will defeat a .30-06 round and gives the entry team a substantial advantage. It takes practice to use the viewing port in a body bunker effectively and even more practice to shoot effectively using the shield; hence, it is important to train with the shield. Ballistic shields are also invaluable should it be necessary to rescue a team member who has been hit or for recovering an injured hostage.

Many teams have developed particular drills using ballistic shields. For example, when moving down a hallway where a threat may be presented from either side, two men can form a V with their shields, with the one on the left holding his pistol in the right hand and the one on the right holding his pistol in the left hand. For moving in an area where the threat may be concentrated on one side, the shields can be used to form an L when moving. For moving where there is a threat from above, a 'turtle' may be formed by putting one shield towards the front and another overhead. Any of these techniques involving movement by two or more shield bearers, however, requires a degree of practice and coordination so that the personnel carrying the ballistic shields can step together for smoothness of advance.

CHOREOGRAPHED ENTRY MANOEUVRES

When it comes to clearing individual rooms, however, a shield can slow down the operation. Choreographed two-man entry manoeuvres such as the buttonhook, cross-button and high/low crossover allow team members quickly to gain control of a room and neutralise any threats encountered (see Diagrams 5.4, 5.5 and 5.6). A point worth noting is that based upon timed experiments by SWAT personnel, of the entry manoeuvres illustrated, the button hook proved the fastest for getting two men through the doorway and into shooting position.

USING LIGHTS

Because the power has often been cut prior to an entry, team members will usually have lights such as the Sure-Fire Tactical Light mounted on their handguns or submachine guns. Some teams also employ gun-mounted Laser sighting devices as an aid to rapid target acquisition. Each of these target acquisition devices, however, requires substantial training in realistic scenarios for most effective use. Laser sights, for example, may not be as effective in rooms which are filled with smoke or gas. On the other hand, in low light, when wearing a gas mask, an under-gun light can be invaluable.

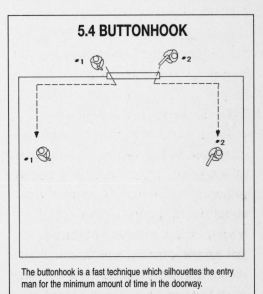

5.4 BUTTONHOOK

The buttonhook is a fast technique which silhouettes the entry man for the minimum amount of time in the doorway.

5.5 CROSS-BUTTON

The Cross-Button is especially effective in situations where a door is located near a wall, thus necessitating that both entry men start from the same side. This is, however, a relatively slow technique.

5.6 HIGH-LOW CROSSOVER (CRISSCROSS)

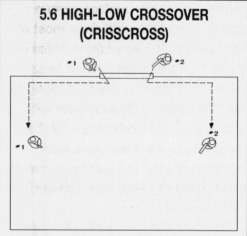

The Crossover has the advantage of allowing each entry man to see into the portion of the room he will enter initially. Once inside the room, he should continue to move into a position to dominate his area of responsibility. To work effectively, the Crossover must be practiced often so the two men can coordinate and not run into each other!

Although each component – negotiator, intelligence analyst, sniper and entry team member – is essential it normally falls to the members of the entry team to carry out a swift and deadly assault when all else has failed and when critical seconds can literally mean life or death to hostages. In a barricade situation, the lives of hostages may not be threatened, but there still exists great danger to the entry team from the barricaded subject, who may well want to die and take as many with him as possible.

When the command to 'Execute! Execute! Execute!' comes over the radio and the entry team follows a stun grenade into a room, the entire operation rides on their training, their teamwork and their precision shooting skills. When an entry team has to earn their pay, this really is a case of, 'Good Guys Wear Black!'

CHAPTER 6

WEAPONS AND EQUIPMENT

Although many hostage rescue units across the world draw most of their basic equipment from police or military stores, most have at least some gear which is specially designed for their mission. This chapter will attempt to give an overview of the most widely used weapons and equipment among hostage rescue units and its tactical employment.

FIREARMS

Any police or military weapon must be highly reliable and capable of instantly stopping the hostile actions of an enemy. Both of these characteristics are also important for weapons used by hostage rescue units. Weapons chosen by hostage rescue teams must also be capable of precision employment since a shot may well have to be taken just inches from a hostage in order to eliminate a hostage-taker. It is also desirable for weapons in use with hostage rescue teams to have the capability of mounting a light, laser or other sighting device to aid the user when operating in low light situations, when gas is employed or in other difficult shooting situations. The hostage rescue weapon must also incorporate excellent safety systems since 'hot' weapons will normally be carried in close proximity to other team members during entries. Although safe, however, the weapon must also allow instant target engagement if necessary. For ease of discussing the missions of different types of firearms and those of most use to hostage rescue units, they will be categorised by type.

HANDGUNS

Although the submachine gun is the primary weapon for most hostage rescue units, there remain two basic **missions** for the handgun.

Primary Usage

For some team members, the handgun will be their primary weapon, chosen because it leaves one hand free for dealing with windows, doors, SWAT cams, stun grenades, or when rappelling, climbing a ladder, etc.. The handgun may also be readily concealed when infiltrating members of a rescue unit into a site (i.e., as maintenance personnel in an office building). Still another situation in which the handgun may be the best choice of weapon is when a team member has to infiltrate a site through very cramped quarters as in an approach through air conditioning or heating ducts.

Secondary Usage

The second mission of the handgun among hostage rescue team members is as a backup to the primary weapon, whether that is a sniping rifle, submachine gun, shotgun, assault rifle or gas gun. Should a malfunction occur with the primary weapon, the team member can just release the shoulder arm, draw his handgun and engage a target. Specialised training ammunition is often used in training to simulate stoppages. The situation may also occur where the primary weapon is inappropriate for a situation. For example, a team member armed with a shotgun encounters a hostage-taker holding a hostage and must take a head shot to stop the hostage-taker. Although specialists such as the Scattergun Technologies Branch of

Wilson Combat can design shotguns capable of patterning a load of buckshot for taking out a hostage-taker with a head shot, normally most shotgunners would release their shotgun and resort to their pistol to take out the hostage-taker.

Suppressed Pistol

Still another handgun mission may occur in specialised circumstances. The use of a suppressed pistol may be called for to eliminate lights during an approach or to eliminate a sentry or dog on a counterterrorist operation. As a result, many hostage rescue teams will have at least one suppressed pistol available.

Realistic Training

Because the handgun is harder to shoot with precision than most shoulder arms, members of hostage rescue teams will normally do a great deal of shooting with their handguns, in excess of 10,000 rounds per year among some units. Both to lend realism and to train personnel better, many of these rounds will be fired in scenarios set in tyre houses or in other specialised range facilities. Training with weapons that allow man-on-man duelling such as the 'Blue' Glocks or H&K SMGs set up for Simunitions (or other weapons designed to allow personnel to engage in training using paint cartridges), allows realistic training as does shooting on video ranges. Whatever the specifics, great stress is put on realistic handgun training for the hostage rescue unit.

Overwhelmingly, hostage rescue units have chosen the autoloading pistol over the revolver, though there have been exceptions, most notably France's RAID or GIGN which have used the excellent Manurhin MR73 revolver. The combination of compactness, weight, magazine capacity and ease of repeat shots normally influences the choice of the auto.

The Hi-Power

For years the most popular handgun among hostage rescue units was the FN/Browning GP or Hi-Power, which was used by the SAS and FBI HRT among others. The Hi-Power combined large magazine capacity (13 rounds of 9x19mm) with proven reliability. It was also the most popular military pistol in the world and was, therefore, available in most military inventories. On the down side, the Hi-Power normally does not have a great trigger pull and until the last decade the sights and safety were, at best, adequate. Nevertheless, the SAS and the FBI HRT were among the well-known units which chose the Hi-Power. FBI Hi-Powers, it should be noted, underwent extensive custom work to enhance their accuracy and reliability.

The Glock

Many hostage rescue units have now replaced the Browning Hi-Power with either the Glock or the SIG. The Glock, which is dominant in the US police market today, is widely used among SWAT teams. The Glock is very reliable and durable and offers good sights, high magazine capacity and, due to the fast action, instant readiness with good safety. The latest generation of Glocks incorporates a rail moulded into the frame which allows the installation of a light or laser aiming device very quickly without unduly affecting the weapon's balance or bulk. The most popular Glock calibres among hostage rescue teams are 9x19mm, .40 S&W and .45

acp. However, the new high velocity .357 SIG round has gained some adherents, and the 10mm round originally developed for the FBI is also available in the Glock. Magazine capacity varies among the most popular Glocks between 13 and 17 rounds, depending on model and calibre.

SIG Pistol

SIG pistols are of very high quality and offer excellent accuracy combined with reliability and high magazine capacity. SIGs for hostage rescue units will generally be chosen in conventional double action format, which allows a fast first shot via a heavier double action pull on the trigger, followed by lighter single action shots on subsequent rounds. With this action, the pistol may be manually cocked on the first round should a precise shot be deemed necessary. The most popular SIG with hostage rescue units is the P-226, though the P-228 or P-229 and the new P-2340 all have their adherents. These pistols are available in 9x19mm, .40 S&W, or .357 SIG calibres. Units preferring the .45 acp round have also chosen the SIG P-220.

AUTHOR'S NOTE

The author's own favourite SIG, the P-210, is an excellent choice for hostage rescue as it is one of the most accurate, reliable and durable autoloading pistols on the market. Only a few units have chosen it, however, due to its single stack magazine, which only holds eight rounds, its single action mechanism and its cost. Still, if one had to make a precision head shot on the hostage-taker, the P-210 would be hard to beat.

The Government Model

With many units in the US, now including the FBI, variations of the Colt Government Model .45 auto are a popular choice. The Government Model offers great possibilities for customising to get better sights, trigger pull and enhanced accuracy. Many gunsmiths specialise in creating customised combat versions of the classic .45, with the author's own favourite being the Gunsite Service Pistol, which is designed for utter reliability and quick combat handling. The Gunsite Service Pistol .45 auto, like the Glock and SIG, comes with night sights to aid in low light shooting. The FBI HRT and a few others units who want large magazine capacity combined with the classic features of the Government Model use the Para-Ordnance, which takes a high capacity 14 round magazine in the full-sized version. With good sights and a smoothed action as well as fitted barrel, the Government Model offers the accuracy required of a hostage rescue unit combined with a sound reputation as a manstopper. It should be noted here, however, that there are loads now available in 9x19mm, .357 SIG, .40 S&W, 10mm and .45 acp with proven ability to stop assailants with one shot well over 90% of the time.

A few units choose other autoloading pistols such as those from Smith & Wesson, Beretta, Ruger, Heckler & Koch, or Walther.

Specialised Pistols

Two other specialised pistols have certain applicability for hostage rescue, one because of the unit which uses it and one because of its chambering. The Heckler & Koch Model Mark 23 SOCOM (Special Operations Command) pistol used by the US Navy SEALs was specifically designed as a handgun for special operations missions. In .45 acp calibre, the Mark 23 is designed to take a suppressor and has a frame allowing the fitting of lasers, flashlights, or other sighting devices. The Mark 23 is a big pistol, but the SEALs train to use it every effectively in hostage rescue situations. It should be noted that the Mark 23's frame with built in rail for lasers or lights has proved such a popular option with hostage rescue teams that the H&K USP, Glock, FN Forty-Nine, SIG PRO, Walther P-99 and other pistols have incorporated this feature. Since the weapon will often be employed in situations where the lights are out, the incorporation of a light or laser may prove absolutely necessary for the degree of precision shot placement needed in hostage rescue operations.

The other specialised pistol is the FN Five-seveN, a military and police pistol with a 20 round magazine and chambered for the 5.7x28mm round also used in FN's P90 SMG. This cartridge fires a light bullet at very high velocity and is excellent for penetrating ballistic vests. Since many terrorists or members of extremist groups have access to body armour, a round which can effectively punch through ballistic material yet is fired from a pistol or compact SMG has a lot of appeal for entry teams.

EXAMPLE

During the rescue carried out by Peruvian special operations forces at the Japanese ambassador's residence in Lima, some members of the rescue team were armed with FN P90s using the 5.7x28mm round to deal with terrorists wearing vests (see Appendix 1).

Other handguns will be encountered in use with police or military units around the world, but their choice will often have been determined by local availability more than specific suitability to the hostage rescue mission. A few units will also allow team members to choose from among a group of two or three pistols those best suited for the specific mission. France's GIGN, for example, used to have Smith & Wesson .44 Magnum

revolvers with bipods available as short-range urban sniping weapons.

'Machine Pistols'

A few other weapons fall between the handgun and the submachine gun. Usually designated machine pistols, these are pistols with the capability of being fired in full auto mode. Generally hard to control, these weapons are not well suited to the hostage rescue mission. Two, however, have achieved some usage with rescue units. In the former USSR some entry teams still use the Stechkin, the select fire 9x18mm machine pistol. With holster stock attached, the Stechkin actually functions as a compact SMG and is about the best machine pistol for hostage rescue. Still, it was most popular with former USSR units because it was the only high-magazine-capacity (20 rounds) pistol in the Soviet inventory. The Glock 18 select fire pistol has also achieved very limited usage with a few hostage rescue units. This weapon can be used much as a standard Glock 17 until a selector switch on the slide is flicked to the full-auto mode, in which case it becomes an automatic weapon. Though surprisingly controllable due to the polymer frame absorbing recoil, this weapon is still not well suited to the hostage rescue mission.

SUBMACHINE GUNS

For many hostage rescue units, the submachine gun, particularly the Heckler & Koch MP-5, has become the signature weapon.

The H&K MP-5

Highly controllable, compact, accurate, able to carry various specialised sighting devices and firing a pistol round which will not risk over-penetration and endanger hostages as much as a rifle round would, the MP-5 is an outstanding hostage rescue weapon. Because of its shoulder stock and pistol grip, the MP-5 offers a more stable shooting platform for precision shot placement. In hostage situations, the entry team member can choose to place the selector on semi-automatic mode rather than on full auto to allow precision placement into a hostage-taker holding or standing near a hostage. Very skilled users have also taught themselves to fire two or three

shot bursts through trigger control to increase shocking effect on the target. Some H&K MP-5s are fitted with a three-shot burst setting on the selector switch. Bursts may be fired at the centre of mass (i.e., the chest area) of a hostage-taker or at the head. If there are indications that the hostage-taker is wearing body armour, then the head shot will definitely be preferable. If body armour is indicated and a head shot is not possible, then a pelvis shot will often cause the hostage-taker to drop and release the hostage. Obviously, the MP-5's accuracy is an important factor in its use by hostage rescue teams.

The versatility of the MP-5 also makes it highly desirable among HRUs. For example, it is available in many configurations including the MP5A2, with fixed stock, normally the most effective for hostage-rescue usage; the MP5A3, with telescoping stock, more compact for infiltrating on to an aircraft, ship, or other venue; the MP5SD, the suppressed ('silenced') version; and the MP5K, the very compact version with front pistol grip. The MP5SD may be used for eliminating lights, dogs, or sentries as was already mentioned in relation to suppressed pistols; however, it also has other tactical advantages. The suppressed weapon, for example, allows entry team members to retain more acute hearing so that they can communicate with each other or hear the cries of hostages. The suppressed version is also invaluable when operating in an environment where chemicals or gasses might be present (i.e., when infiltrating a site through underground sewers) since the suppressor lowers muzzle flash which might ignite flammable chemicals or gasses. Note that specialised 'wet' suppressors are even more effective for this application. The MP5K, though only about 13 inches in overall length, can be shot quite effectively with practice due to the front pistol grip and folding stock. However, it is rarely chosen by hostage rescue units due to the availability of the more easily mastered MP5A2. Some operators like the front pistol grip well enough that they add it to the MP5A2 or A3.

The Uzi

Though the MP-5 dominates among SMGs in service with military or police units charged with hostage rescue, there are other good SMGs which also see some usage. Probably the most widely used pistol-calibre SMG, after the MP-5, is the Uzi. Known for its durability, the Uzi has proved particularly popular with combat swimmer units which also have a hostage rescue mission. Generally, closed-bolt SMGs such as the H&K MP-5 have been considered more accurate, which limited the Uzi which fired from an open bolt. However, the most recent version of the Uzi fires from a closed bolt as well. Among the well-known hostage rescue units which have used the Uzi are, of course, the Israelis, as well as the Royal Dutch Marines and the Peruvian unit which carried out the rescue at the Japanese Embassy. The Peruvians, in fact, used Mini-Uzis, a more compact version of the Uzi.

The Italian Beretta M12 has also been used, while the Ruger MP9, which has many characteristics in common with the Uzi, has been adopted by some US SWAT teams. Some US SWAT teams have also used the 9mm version of the Colt AR-15/M-16.

EXAMPLE

The recent FN P90 5.7mm SMG has also attracted some interest because of its ability to punch through ballistic vests. It was also used by Peruvian Commandos during the operation at the Japanese ambassador's residence in Lima to eliminate terrorists wearing ballistic vests.

Rifle Calibre SMGs

Some HRUs have also found rifle-calibre SMGs – sometimes termed 'short-carbines' – invaluable because of the greater penetration and range they grant, while remaining compact. However, there is also the increased danger of a round over penetrating and killing a hostage after passing through a hostage-taker. Among the best of these rifle-calibre SMGs are the Russian AKSU 'Krinkov', the H&K 53 and the Colt CAR-15. Since these short-barreled weapons normally have greater muzzle flash and recoil, it takes even more practice to become expert with them.

ASSAULT RIFLES

The assault rifle, though in the arsenals of most hostage rescue units, is perhaps the least applicable weapon for this mission. Designed to grant an infantryman the ability to deliver overwhelming firepower during an advance, the assault rifle is not really well-suited to the surgical mission of hostage rescue. The most likely employment for the assault rifle is as a weapon for the observer of a sniper/observer team or as a short-range countersniping rifle for members of the perimeter team. The assault rifle may also be employed on certain counterterrorist operations where it is expected that the terrorists will be wearing high-threat-level body armour or when there may be the need to take shots through some type of cover (i.e., through the partition in a train compartment). In some units, an M-16 with M-203 grenade launcher is issued to the team member designated to deploy gas, in which case the M-16 normally serves as his primary weapon as well. In some cases, the assault rifle may also be used because it is the only weapon available. In some parts of the world, hostage rescue units have been equipped with the AK-47 because it is the universal weapon within their country's arsenal. Some US Military Police Special Reaction Teams (SRTs) have also been equipped with the M-16 for the hostage rescue mission.

Use in Entries

If specialised frangible ammunition (which will be discussed under 'Ammunition') is chosen, then the assault rifle can function quite adequately for entries. One assault rifle which has seen some hostage rescue use offers a particular degree of versatility. The Bullpup Steyr AUG is very compact and, hence, may be handled as easily as an SMG during an entry. A 9mm conversion unit is available which allows a quick switch from a .223 assault rifle to a 9mm SMG. The advantage of this system is that a soldier or police officer can be trained on one weapon which may be used for a wide variety of situations. The availability of 9mm or .223 CAR-15s offers this same versatility.

SNIPING RIFLES

Because of its ability to end a hostage situation quickly and surgically, many consider the sniping rifle the most valuable weapon in the armoury of the hostage rescue unit. Certainly, it ranks with the handgun and SMG in importance.

Selection

When selecting a sniping rifle for the hostage rescue mission, primary consideration must be given to its accuracy, though weight must also be a factor since the sniper must be able to carry the rifle into position, often after a fairly arduous stalk or climb. The basic standard for most sniping rifles is the ability to shoot a minute of angle (one inch for each 100 yards) out to 300 yards. Most of the better sniping rifles will achieve 1/2 MOA or even better. 7.62mm NATO (.308) is the standard sniping calibre throughout the western world, though calibres such as .300 Winchester or .338 Lapua are often used for longer shots. Some urban SWAT teams also use .223 calibre sniping rifles, but the higher sensitivity to cross wind and poorer performance on intermediate barriers make the .223 a poor choice compared to the .308. In Russia and former Soviet Republics, the 7.62x54R remains the standard sniping round.

Although there are dozens of excellent sniping rifles available, a few are so ubiquitous that they should be mentioned.

Bolt Action Sniping Rifles

Perhaps the most widely used sniping rifle among Western HRUs has been Steyr's SSG. Now in service for over three decades, the SSG has established an outstanding reputation for accuracy and ease of usage. Its use of detachable box magazines has contributed to this popularity since it offers the sniper the ability to change quickly the type of ammunition if so desired or to reload easily. Among US police SWAT teams, the Remington 700 has established its reputation for accuracy combined with lightness and reasonable cost. The Light Tactical Rifle (LTR) which incorporates a fluted 20 inch barrel is especially easy to carry or deploy in cramped quarters

yet does not suffer in accuracy. Even more compact is the folding stock sniping rifle built on the Remington 700 action by Robar. This rifle may be ordered with barrels of 16 inches or even shorter and with folded stock may be easily transported into position by the sniper. Yet, the Robar will readily shoot sub-MOA groups. The US military M24 sniping system used by some military counterterrorist units is also based on the Remington 700.

Considered by many the world's best sniping rifle, the Accuracy International PM (L96A1 in British military designation) will shoot sub-MOA groups to 500 yards or beyond and with a truly competent shooter can score 1/2 MOA groups at 500 yards. Very well designed ergonomically, the PM allows most tactical marksmen to maximise their skills. This is the only rifle, for example, with which the author has ever been able to shoot below one MOA at over 300 yards. Accuracy International also offers larger calibre rifles for long-range usage, including .330 Winchester Magnum, .338 Lapua and even .50 Browning MG.

Self-Loading Sniping Rifles

These three are typical of the best of the bolt action sniping rifles available to HRUs; however, some units prefer a self-loading sniping rifle which allows faster follow-up shots. The Russian Dragunov, for example, uses a semi-automatic action and a ten round magazine to allow very rapid engagement of multiple targets. Heckler & Koch's PSG-1 is another semi-automatic design which has achieved substantial acceptance in the counterterrorist community, although its heaviness is considered a slight disadvantage. Among US law enforcement agencies, the Springfield Armoury semi-auto M21 sniping rifle based on the M-14 rifle has been popular when a self-loading sniping rifle has been deemed desirable.

Suppressed Sniping Rifles

For highly specialised situations, suppressed sniping rifles are available, though their use of subsonic ammunition normally limits their range substantially. The Russian VSS Silent Sniping Rifle uses a 9x39mm cartridge and is specifically designed as a short range silent killer. Since the VSS is select fire and uses ten or 20 round magazines, it allows very fast follow up shots, an advantage since its quietness might allow multiple terrorists to be taken out before they realised a sniper was shooting at them.

Optics

As important as the sniping rifle itself is, its optics are equally important. The tactical riflescope should present a combination of durability, light-gathering capability, range estimating aid and ease of windage and elevation adjustment. Many tactical marksmen prefer a variable scope which allows adjustment of magnification somewhere between 2.5X and 12X to fit the tactical situation. Precise windage and elevation adjustments are very important, preferably allowing adjustment in 1/4 MOA increments. There are different within-the-lens range estimation systems. The author prefers the Mil Dot system which has already been discussed in Chapter 4 on sniping. Illuminated reticles which aid in low light shooting are also a desirable feature. Perhaps most important of all, though, is the quality of the lenses which allow a very clear sight picture at varying ranges.

As with sniping rifles, there is a wide selection of excellent optics. Within the US SWAT community, Leupold's Tactical Scopes are highly thought of and offer an excellent compromise between reasonable price, durability and precision. Among European sniping scopes, Schmidt & Bender, Kahles and Zeiss have especially good reputations. The Rumanian firm IOR Valdada has recently achieved substantial success in marketing its tactical scopes as well. Famed for its durability, the Russian PSO-1 is the standard on the Dragunov.

The mating of the proper optical sight with the sniping rifle is highly critical and requires selection of the proper base, rings, scope covers and other components along with a bipod, usually from Harris, to create an integrated precision shooting system.

SHOTGUNS
Uses

The shotgun is often misunderstood when used in the hostage rescue mission since many think of it as a weapon which throws out a broad pattern of shot as likely to hit hostages as hostage-takers. First, most tactical shotguns actually throw a relatively tight pattern of buckshot at the range at which they are likely to be employed during an entry. If choked by Scattergun Technologies or the The Shotgun Shop, they throw an even tighter pattern and, in an emergency, can actually be used to take a head shot on a hostage-taker when a hostage is nearby. This is not an advisable practice and requires great precision – normally the shooter will aim at the eye socket away from the hostage, thus keeping the spread of the pattern within the hostage-taker's head. However, the use of the shotgun as an actual rescue weapon rarely occurs. Instead, the shotgun is used to blow locks or hinges off of doors and to allow the 'tail gunner' to protect the rest of the team by covering areas such as hallways or stairwells which might disgorge hostage-takers. Often shotguns used to blow doors or locks have a 'stand off device specifically designed to position the weapon for 'door busting'. Once again, the shotgun will only be used in an emergency to deal with hostage-takers holding hostages nearby.

Shotguns in Use

The most common shotgun in use around the world with HRUs is the Remington 870 slide-action 12 gauge. Proved on the streets with US law enforcement agencies for decades, the 870 is an outstanding combat shotgun. The Mossberg 590 slide-action shotgun is also widely used. Among self-loading shotguns, the Remington 11-87 Police model and the Benelli M1 are the most popular choice. However, since the shotgun used by hostage rescue personnel may be employed with special less lethal munitions or lock-busting rounds that might not function as a self-loading action, the slide-action is generally preferred. Under-barrel lights are available for shotguns and will most likely be attached to those weapons used by entry teams. At least

some entry teams use a short-barrelled shotgun—14 inch or even less-- equipped with a pistol grip to bust doors. However, such altered shotguns are far more difficult to control and are much less effective if used in the anti-personnel role. Many shotgunners use a three-point sling for their weapon, which allows them to release it as soon as they've taken off hinges or locks, then draw their handgun in case it is necessary to engage a suspect.

AMMUNITION

With hundreds of different loadings available in such popular counterterrorist calibres as 9x19mm and .308, only a quick overview can be given here of ammunition chosen for the hostage rescue mission. Much of the research in specialised ammunition for snipers and entry teams has been directed at two seemingly mutually exclusive characteristics--the ability to penetrate intermediate barriers or ballistic vests without over-penetrating or ricocheting and endangering hostages. Loads which deliver the maximum portion of the shock effect within the targeted individual are also desirable.

SPECIAL PURPOSE AMMO FOR HANDGUNS AND SMGS

Among the special purpose ammo developed for handguns and SMGs, rounds which combine stopping power with penetration and frangibility have received a great deal of interest. The recently introduced RBCD Platinum Plus loadings, for example, claim to combine all three desirable features. The 37 grain bullet of the .40 S&W load achieves a muzzle velocity of 2,550 feet per second and is capable of defeating the types of soft body armour most likely to be used by terrorists, yet it remains frangible and delivers substantial energy into the target. The .45 grain .45 acp ExpHP from the same company travels at 2,550 feet per second as well, while the 28 grain .357 SIG bullet leaves the muzzle at 2,820 feet per second.

Another solution to the problem of delivering massive stopping effect without over-penetration or ricochet has been marketed by Cor-Bon with the BeeSafe load or by loads from MagSafe or Glaser. Glaser, the original developer of the Safety Slug type of load, uses small shot bonded together so that the projectile hits the target with the energy of the heavier weight, then expends the energy within the wound as the small shot breaks free. The BeeSafe and MagSafe offer variations on this basic design. This type of ammunition is especially desirable aboard aircraft or in other situations (i.e., an assault in a chemical plant or nuclear facility) where the danger of collateral damage is high.

Countering Ricochet

Both Winchester and Remington offer frangible ammunition for assaults where ricochet could be a problem--aboard a steel ship, for example. Winchester's bullet is a composite of tungsten powder, copper powder and nylon resin, while Remington uses a powdered iron core. Both are very well-designed, but in testing the Winchester load the author found that it would be a mistake to assume that because it is frangible it will not penetrate walls during an assault in a building. Care must still be taken where the bullet is fired!

Stopping Power

Many of the premier ammunition manufacturers offer loads specifically designed to combine accuracy with a high degree of stopping power for use by SWAT or counterterrorist personnel. Among the best of these handgun loads are Black Hills' moly-coated rounds, Federal's Tactical Handgun loads, Hornady's Extreme Terminal Performance (XTP) loads, Remington's Golden Saber, Speer's Gold Dot and Winchester's Partition Gold. Winchester also makes subsonic rounds specifically designed for use in suppressed weapons which retain good stopping power through the use of a heavier bullet at the subsonic velocity.

One of the most interesting of the European specialised counterterrorist loads is the GECO Blitz Action Trauma (BAT) 9x19mm round. Designed to give good stopping power yet function with utter reliability in SMGs, the BAT round uses an 86 grain solid copper hollow point with a black plastic ball filling the hollow to aid reliability. This ball falls out of the cavity after the bullet leaves the barrel. The author has used this round extensively and has found it excellent. GSG-9 has found, too, that this round is much more effective on vehicle tyres than most 9mm loads.

One other handgun load which should be mentioned is the 115 grain 9mm +P+ load from Federal or Remington. Designed specially for law enforcement or military personnel, this load gives the 9mm great stopping power yet retains excellent accuracy.

SPECIAL PURPOSE AMMO FOR TACTICAL RIFLES

Loads for tactical rifles have many of the same conflicting requirements as handgun ammunition; however, for the sniper, accuracy usually outweighs other considerations. As a result, the very accurate .308 match loads from Black Hills and Federal are widely used by hostage rescue sharpshooters. Federal also offers its line of Tactical Rifle loads in .223 and .308. These loads combine match-grade precision with the ability to penetrate intermediate barriers. However, the author has found that these loads do not normally shoot anywhere near the point of impact of

Federal match ammo of the same bullet weight; hence, any sniper using Tactical loads must be sure to sight the rifle specifically for them. On the very positive side, Federal's .308 Tactical loads perform much better than most other police rounds through glass, even aircraft glass.

Consideration has also been given to tactical rifle ammunition which does not ricochet or over-penetrate. Winchester, for example, offers a 33 grain frangible load in .223 calibre, while Federal offers its Blitz round which is also designed for frangibility. These loads are especially popular with HRUs which assault with the M-16 or AUG in .223. Hornady has a round designated the Tactical Application Police (TAP) in .223 and .308 which is less likely to over-penetrate or ricochet. It is also intended to deliver all its energy into the target for great killing power.

DOOR-BREAKING MUNITIONS

Special purpose door-breaking or lock-eliminating shotgun loads are among the most important special purpose munitions for hostage rescue teams. The

MK Ballistic Systems' 'Master Key' is a good example. With a 30 gram projectile composed of fine metal held together in a matrix fired at 1,560 feet per second, on impact this round becomes a fine powder which creates less possibility of harming hostages within the site or members of the entry team. It is important that entry team members wear goggles to prevent eye injury from such rounds. The Master Key will normally remove the hinges or lock bolts on wooden doors with one shot, though metal doors might require a second shot. Generally, the Master Key is most effective against lock bolts when fired at 90 degrees from about three inches, while against hinges a 30 degree up or down angle is most effective, but also fired from three inches. Another round which has always been popular for taking off locks or hinges is the 'Shok-Lok', also known with police humour as 'Avon Calling'. Some companies offer a stand off shotgun adapter for use with special purpose door-busting loads. The Master Key may also be used against car doors.

For anti-personnel usage, however, most SWAT or hostage rescue units prefer Federal's Tactical shotgun loads which have lighter recoil, thus allowing faster shotgun handling and greater accuracy. For situations such as stopping a vehicle, MK Ballistics Systems offers special purpose loads such as their Enhanced Penetration Slug and their QB (Quadrangle Buckshot) slug. The latter also works very well against electrical equipment, the pie-shaped projectiles ripping wiring to shreds.

In simple terms, ammunition for the hostage rescue team is designed to deliver the maximum stopping effect upon the hostage-taker while creating the minimum amount of danger for the hostages. Modern bullet design has allowed development of some excellent loads which accomplish this dual mission extremely well.

CHEMICAL MUNITIONS

LAUNCHING

Chemical munitions, often generically termed 'tear gas', may be launched in various manners. Standard 12 gauge shotguns may be used to fire 12 gauge chemical munitions. There are also grenade launchers which may be fitted to 12 gauge shotguns, thus allowing chemical grenades to be launched by firing a 12 gauge blank. Companies such as Defense Technology Corporation of America, Sage International, Heckler & Koch and Federal Laboratories make specific 37/38mm and 40mm chemical launchers specifically designed to deploy this munitions. The M-203 grenade launcher for the M-16 rifle may also be used in 37mm or 40mm format.

TYPES AVAILABLE

Just to give an overview of the types of chemical munitions available, Advanced Material Laboratory and DEFTEC, among others, offer 12 gauge shotgun rounds loaded with CS and/or CN and able to penetrate barriers. The Advanced Materials Laboratory 12 gauge round may be fired accurately to 75 metres.

A greater variety of 37 and 40mm grenades are available. Advanced

Materials Laboratory offers Liquid Barricade Projectiles, which are fin-stabilised for accuracy and liquid-filled, thus eliminating the danger of fire. These rounds disperse their contents upon impact. DEFTEC offers similar munitions in 37mm and 40mm, but also offers a 37/38mm Heavy Barricade round with a weighted tip designed to penetrate heavy doors, windows or walls, as well as trailer sidings. This round may be fired to about 100 yards accurately. However, because it is longer than most 37mm chemical rounds, it may have to be fired from a DEFTEC chemical launcher. There is also a substantial threat of secondary fires with this projectile.

One of the most widely used chemical munitions in barricade situations is the DEFTEC Ferret Liquid-filled Barricade Round. This round offers little likelihood of secondary fires, yet retains the ability to penetrate hollow-core doors, windows, etc.. It disperses upon impact. The Ferret round is also offered in powder-filled configuration. The DEFTEC 12 gauge round is offered in both liquid and powder forms, as well.

Munitions launched from grenade launchers affixed to a rifle or a shotgun barrel and employing a blank round are also used. Among companies making such munitions are Dynamit Nobel.

DISTRACTION AND DIVERSIONARY DEVICES

Distraction devices are used to give an entry team a few seconds advantage in confronting a hostage-taker or barricaded suspect. Such devices generally produce between 165 and 185 decibels of sound, 2.5-7.5 million candlepower of flash and a certain amount of over pressure within the area. Over pressure normally runs in the range of 3.0-5.0 psi, a range that will result in 1% of the population suffering ear damage. This combination normally disorients the hostage-taker and the hostage by contracting pupils, causing ringing in the ears and creating confusion to allow the entry team to get into the room and either subdue a suspect or shoot a hostage-taker before he can harm the hostage. The disorientation of the hostage may also be a positive aspect since it often prevents the hostage from panicking and moving into the line of fire. It is important, too, that the entry team follow up the distraction device very quickly, normally within one to two seconds.

EFFECTIVE USAGE

To be most effective, it is best if a distraction device is deployed in a darkened room; hence, the tactic of cutting electricity before an assault. Distraction devices are usually more effective in enclosed areas which contain their effects. However, great care must be taken in deploying them in such areas, especially if small babies, who might be severely injured by the over pressure, or hostages with heart problems are present. It must be considered, as well, that children are likely to panic and run away from the rescue team, often into the arms of the hostage-taker; hence, great care must be taken about using distraction devices during entries at schools. Distraction devices are most effective if they detonate while in the air in the

middle of a room. If the device should become trapped between a subject and a wall or other solid object it can cause serious injury or death. If the device should land amidst small objects (i.e., nuts and bolts in a machine shop), they can become projectiles when the device goes off. Distraction devices may also set off smoke detectors, creating a substantial amount of additional noise which can distract team members if they do not expect it.

DEPLOYMENT

Most entry teams use pull-pin detonated grenades. Some prefer multi-detonation devices which deploy sub munitions as they go off, thus lengthening and increasing the effect. Another popular form of distraction device may be launched from a 12 gauge shotgun or a 37 or 40mm launcher. Still another device is of a strip type designed to be slid under a door and then set off. These strip devices are often used as a combination distraction and diversionary device if the entry team is coming in through another point of entry.

One of the more popular distraction devices is the DEFTEC #25. DEFTEC also produces the compact Omni Blast 100 which may readily be carried in pockets on the assault vest. Still another model from DEFTEC is the #15 Stinger Grenade which combines flash powder with 180 rubber balls. However, since the rubber balls are hurled with some force, this device would not normally be used when hostages are present. MK Ballistic Systems makes various distraction devices designated 'Thor's Hammer'. NICO Pyrotechnik has numerous devices as well, including a 'seven-bang' device for teams which prefer the multi-detonation munitions.

Hand-thrown devices utilise a lever which the operator holds down after removing the safety pin. A solid grip is important until the instant the device is hurled into the room. Most of the companies which make distraction devices actually offer training seminars for 'grenadiers' to teach them to use the devices effectively and safely.

DIVERSIONARY DEVICES

Although many use the terms 'distraction device' and 'diversionary device' interchangeably, the latter is sometimes classified as a separate entity which uses flash, sound, smoke, or other methods to draw a hostage-taker's attention away from a point of entry.

NIGHT VISION DEVICES

As so many entries are carried out in low-light situations, devices which enable the operator to see more effectively in the dark grant him a great advantage. Military hostage rescue units normally have access to more sophisticated night vision equipment than civilian police agencies, unless those agencies are units such as the FBI HRT or French GIGN which function as the national counterterrorist unit.

There are two primary types of night vision optics available for hostage rescue operations.

SELF-CONTAINED DEVICES

One type is the night vision goggle

which normally incorporates its own infrared illuminator. These have the advantage of being self-contained and may be used without the mounting of special equipment on the weapon, though they are most effective if an infrared aimer is affixed and sighted to the weapon. Using this system, as soon as the aiming point is illuminated on the target and spotted through the infrared goggles, the operator may take his shot. On the downside, night vision goggles generally require substantial training to use well and severely limit the operator's field of view. For example, two of the most widely used goggles in the US – the Night Vision Equipment Company AN/PVS-5C and the AN/PVS-7B – limit vision to 40 degrees.

MOUNTED DEVICES

Night vision systems mounted on the weapon must be a trade-off between technology and bulk. One of the most popular night vision optical sights is the Raptor, designed primarily for use by snipers. Designed to intensify available starlight, moonlight or city glow, the Raptor incorporates an illuminated red reticle as an additional aid to precision shooting.

Because the technology of night optics is constantly improving it is difficult to give specifications of the current state of the art equipment. As a rule of thumb, however, each new generation of sights provides greater image intensification with a smaller sighting device.

BODY ARMOUR

Although it is currently impossible to offer a member of an entry team full ballistic protection without limiting his freedom of action, through the use of Kevlar and other modern bullet resistant materials, it is possible to increase greatly his chance of surviving a shot from a hostage-taker or barricaded suspect. This protection is normally provided for entry team members through a combination of a ballistic helmet and a tactical ballistic vest, which not only contains Kevlar and ceramic or metal bullet resistant materials but also incorporates load carrying pockets and pouches. Many of the current generation of assault vests use inserts of Spectra, a polyethylene fibre which is very light but grants ten times the protection level of steel on a weight-to-weight basis. These two basic items may be supplemented with ballistic goggles, Kevlar balaclavas, ballistic crotch protectors and ballistic leg guards.

BALLISTIC VEST

The most basic item of protection is the ballistic vest since it covers the vital organs. Many armed subjects will also shoot at the 'centre of mass', the torso, thus making protection critical. Ballistic vests are normally rated for their resistance to different ballistic threats. The relatively light Kevlar vests worn under many police patrol officers' uniforms, for example, are rated to stop handgun ammunition such as 9x19mm. Such vests generally carry a rating of Threat Level II or IIA. The assault vest, however, must be able to stop a rifle calibre round. Such vests are rated Threat Level IIIA or IV (with an insert).

A good example is the FN assault vest designed to stop 5.56 NATO rounds. Ballistic material comprises 24 layers of Kevlar plus a 6.5mm steel plate. The FN vest rated to stop

7.62x39MM uses the same number of layers of Kevlar but only a 5mm steel plate. Because rifle bullets can cause severe blunt trauma even if the assault vest prevents their penetration, many vests have some type of trauma attenuation pad on the inside. Frequently, when a fatal shot occurs to an entry team member, it is because the bullet manages to hit at a point where there is a gap in the armour, such as under the arm. As a result, the fit of the ballistic vest is critical and great care must be taken that ceramic or metal plates do not shift from their proper position.

Among the other features incorporated into many ballistic assault vests are Nomex fire-resistant outer shells, sewn-in channels for radio wires, velcro identification panels across the front of the vest, ballistic collar and groin protection and a choice of colours. Note that the identification panels are important in some situations so that anyone encountered while clearing a building can instantly tell they are facing law enforcement personnel.

AUTHOR'S NOTE

An interesting note on ballistic vests is that models are available for canine members of SWAT teams as well as human members.

HELMET

After the ballistic vest, the most important element of the entry man's ballistic protection is his helmet. Not only must the entry team helmet provide ballistic protection, however. It must also allow the use of goggles or a gas mask and radio equipment. Ballistic face masks are available for the most widely used ballistic helmets. A good example of such a ballistic helmet is Protech's Delta Forces model which is constructed of a Spectra composite and will stop 9x19mm bullets.

OTHER PROTECTIVE GEAR

Other assault gear designed to protect the team members includes gloves designed to protect the hands while rappelling or containing Nomex for those who may be dealing with diversionary devices. Many team members also wear elbow and knee pads to protect themselves from door frames, window

frames, furniture or other objects encountered during a dynamic entry. Some teams, instead, wear padded underwear of the type designed for motorcycle racers. Nomex hoods or other Nomex clothing may be worn if the danger of fire is considered high. Boots are normally chosen to protect the feet while allowing ease of movement during rappelling or climbing. Some teams wear boots with a metal insert in the sole to protect the foot from spiked booby traps or other sharp objects.

BALLISTIC SHIELD

One other item of ballistic protection which has proved invaluable during entries is the Body Bunker or Ballistic Shield. Designed to offer a portable ballistic wall with a vision port, the Ballistic Shield is used by the first man through the door in entries where it is highly likely that an armed suspect will be immediately encountered. Many shields are also equipped with lights which illuminate a room as the point man moves into it. The most portable ballistic shields, which weigh in the 14-18lb range, normally give protection against 9x19mm ammunition; however, heavier shields such as the

PROTECH NATO High Threat Ballistic Shield can stop up to 7.62x39mm rounds. In the UK the National Plastics Shield is widely issued by police entry teams. Offering even greater ballistic protection is PROTECH's Phoenix IV which gives protection against armour-piercing bullets. However, this shield is so heavy that it is mounted on rollers.

Entry team members must train in shooting techniques using the shield as the ability to score hits while peeking around a shield must be developed through extensive training. Those using ballistic shields during entries are also slowed because of the need to remain behind the shield. It is important, too, that team members be constantly reminded that the shield does not protect them from threats above.

ENTRY TOOLS

One of the first rules those on entry teams learn is to check doors before ramming them. It's amazing how often they are actually unlocked! Given the fact,

however, that it will frequently be necessary to force an entry, then those on hostage rescue teams have many choices, both human and machine-powered.

The human-powered tools have the advantage of making little noise until the door is actually being forced open, are less expensive and more portable.

Machine-powered entry devices have the advantage of allowing great force to be applied to heavy doors or windows.

Breaching may also be carried out with explosives, an option which will be discussed later in this chapter.

DOORS

Typically, doors fall into two categories: those which open inward and those which open outward. Those which open inward will normally be attacked with a ram, while those which open outward will generally fall to a pry bar or some other ripping tool. Some SWAT teams use a ram, usually between three and four feet in length and between 25-50lbs in weight, for the inward opening doors and a set of fireman's breaching tools, consisting of a pry axe and ram bar, for outward opening doors. Rams must be balanced so that one man can apply sufficient force to the door to take it down quickly. They must also be short enough that they can be deployed in a confined space. Still, the 'ram man' on most tactical or SWAT teams will usually be a large, muscular individual. To give an idea of a couple of typical rams, the B-SAFE SupRam-It is designed for use in confined spaces. Only 30 inches long and 35lbs in weight, it generates 19,000 foot pounds of kinetic force. The larger B-SAFE SupRam-It II is 40 inches long, weighs 50lbs and generates 26,000 foot pounds of kinetic force. Special backpacks to carry entry tools are often used.

THE ENTRY TOOL PACKAGE

Companies which supply entry teams with equipment often offer a package of entry tools which might consist of: ram, pry-bar, sledge hammer and bolt cutters. A pry bar incorporating various functions and extremely popular with entry teams is the 'Hooligan Tool'. Basically, a pickax with a flat blade at the other end, the Hooligan Tool is the 'Swiss Army Knife' of entry tools. Another option popular with

many entry teams is the B-SAFE Omni Jamb Spreader, a hydraulic jack which quietly spreads a door jam to allow an inward-opening door to swing open. For heavy, fortified doors, more powerful models are available, with the Hydra-Force III being compact yet generating 10,000 pounds per square inch of pressure. Hurst Entry Systems offers a wide range of powered entry tools with the option of hooking them to electric, gas or hand operated power units. Among the most useful is the Maverick, which weighs 38lbs and may be used for powered spreading, pulling or cutting.

GRATINGS AND BARS

Since entry teams sometimes encounter sites which have been heavily barricaded with gratings or bars, breaching hooks which can be affixed, then attached to a vehicle may be used to pull the grate or bar loose. Not only can these be useful in situations where the hostage-taker has placed such obstacles, but bars or grates may also be encountered in hostage incidents at jewellery stores, gun shops, banks or other businesses where security of the site is a concern.

FENCES

One other interesting device, though not strictly used for entry, is the Tactical Fence Climber from Tactical and Survival Specialities, Inc.. Based on the premise that even very physically fit, rescue team members will not have the agility easily to get over fences wearing 40lbs or more of body armour and assault gear while carrying a ram or long arm, the Climber uses V's with extensions at the top of each leg of the V. By poking this device through chain link fences, the entry team member is supplied with steps to ascend and descend a fence.

USE OF EXISTING STRUCTURES

Whichever entry tools are chosen, the operators will become much more proficient with practice. As a result, it is useful if an entry team can arrange with construction companies that demolish buildings to allow them to practise in structures awaiting demolition. Normally, if the building is due for destruction anyway, there will be no problem in ripping and ramming doors throughout the building. Many industrial buildings will also incorporate some heavy-duty doors

which will offer a challenge to the entry team. Such buildings are also useful for practicing various other skills. For example, room-clearing techniques can be practised in low light in conjunction with ramming or prying doors.

EXPLOSIVE ENTRY MATERIAL

Either for speed, because the optimum point of entry is through a wall, or because a door is heavily fortified, it may be necessary to carry out an explosive entry. Among the points at which explosive entry charges may be effectively used are: • wooden doors, • steel doors, • barred doors as in prisons, • windows, • glass doors, • internal walls, • to create shooting ports through walls or doors, • masonry walls and • sheet metal walls.

Entry Charges

Some agencies – particularly military special operations units with the hostage rescue mission – have their own demolition experts who construct specialised entry charges. However, there are also specially designed commercial charges for explosive breaching available to law enforcement or military agencies. These include specialised door cutting charges, which combine detonating cord in a soft foam flexible frame. The charge may be attached over the hinges to blow the door or around an area to blow a hole – through a wall, for example – to make a firing port. One of the easiest types of explosive to deploy is Foamex, which is supplied in an aerosol can.

Silhouette Charge

Many entry teams also use what is known as a silhouette charge which involves wrapping detonating cord around a standard silhouette shooting target. This prefabricated, or on-site-fabricated, charge may then be placed at the point where the explosive entry will be carried out and detonated. Normally, detonation will be via an electronic blasting cap, though explosive entry technicians are also familiar with safety or time fuses as well. The breaching charge is then wired into a blasting machine of some type. Frequently, in the US military and police community, the Claymore Firing Device will be used. Various explosives have been used by entry teams, but C4 is normally considered one of the best, if not *the* best, choice.

Water Charge

Many teams like to use what is called a 'water charge'. Combining a container of water with detonator cord, this entry device is suspended against the door or wall, then detonated. By limiting blast and fragmentation, this type of charge allows an entry team to follow up the breaching charge even more quickly.

Window Charge

Another specialised type of charge is the window charge, which, unlike a door cutting charge, is designed to push. Instead of detonating cord, the window charge is usually constructed of crushed TNT.

Obviously, explosive entry is an invaluable tool in hostage rescue; however, the employment of explosives for breaching is a highly specialised skill. No team should attempt explosive breaching without having well-trained personnel available. On at least some US SWAT teams, the bomb squad comes under the same command as the SWAT team and one or more bomb technicians respond to situations where an explosive entry might be deemed desirable to lend their expertise. Other teams send one or more members to receive explosive breaching training.

TACTICAL OBSERVATION AND INTELLIGENCE GATHERING EQUIPMENT

Knowing what hostage-takers are doing and where they and their hostages are located within a site allows an entry team to plan most effectively for a rescue. Such information may be gleaned from various sources.

MICROPHONES

Sensitive microphones may be placed in air conditioning or heating ducts, inserted through vents, or threaded through small holes which have been drilled for them. For especially tight spaces such as keyholes a tube microphone may be inserted. If multiple microphones can be placed within a site, they can often be used to locate his and his hostage's position by the strength of the signals when he or the hostage is talking. When members of the rescue team can infiltrate into an apartment or office next to the hostage site, then the electronic stethoscope may also be employed. In optimum conditions, parabolic microphones or laser microphones which pick up sounds from window glass may be used.

FIBRE OPTICS

Video systems may also be employed. Small fibre optic lenses of the types used for microsurgery can be inserted through pinholes or vents. Many entry teams now make extensive use of what may generically be called SWAT cams. These are video cameras mounted on a wand which can be extended past doorways or windows to show an image on a screen mounted just above the grip of the camera. SWAT cams allow an entry team to examine a room without exposing themselves, thus lessening their own danger but also that for hostages since they can determine the tactical situation before entering. The 'low-tech' version of the SWAT cam is the folding inspection mirror which may be extended to look into a room. Many point men on entry teams are equipped with such mirrors. Another useful video device is a camera designed to be used in conjunction with a Leupold tactical rifle scope, thus allowing members of an entry team or those in the command post to see what the sniper sees.

RADAR

Thanks to Hughes Missile Systems, entry rescue units have access to a compact Motion Detection Radar – the MDR-1. This unit, which only weighs 16lbs and has a ten hour battery pack, allows the detection of motion through nonmetallic walls. The MDR-1 is good out to 200 feet in the open, but when 'seeing' through walls, composition and thickness can affect results. For example, the MDR-1 can detect motion at 15 feet through three feet of concrete blocks. The MDR-1 is invaluable in situations where the location of the hostage-takers and hostages within a room or building is unknown. Prior to an explosive breach, for example, determination can be made where possible threats will be encountered within a room and whether any hostages will be endangered by blowing a wall or door. The MDR-1 can

also help to determine the best point of entry and where distraction devices can best be deployed.

MISCELLANEOUS PERSONAL EQUIPMENT

CARRIERS AND POUCHES

The member of a hostage rescue team must balance the need for ease of movement versus the possibility of needing specialised equipment during an operation. As a result, his assault vest and other webbed gear carry an assortment of useful accessories. The actual assault vest is normally designed to carry the body armour within, though some vests are designed to be worn over body armour. Most vests are designed to be modular so that each individual team member can carry gear that fits his mission. For example, magazine pouches for shotgun, submachine gun or rifle may be affixed. The vest also has a carrier, usually on the back, for the radio. Other items which may be carried on the vest are the handgun, stun grenades, first aid items, handcuffs or flex cuffs, a tactical knife and gas mask.

KNIFE

Some mention should be made of the knife since it is a highly useful tool for cutting free hostages or dealing with numerous other contingencies. Many entry team members actually carry a small utility knife or tool such as the Swiss Army Knife, Leatherman Tool, or SOG Tool Clip and a larger utility knife with a four to six inch blade for heavier cutting tasks. The author had a custom blade made to wear on his tactical vest. Designated a Tactical Entry Tool, this knife incorporates sharp edges for cutting with a blunt heavy-duty tip for prying. It is also designed so that it can be used to strip wires or perform other general tasks.

HOLSTERS, HARNESSES AND BELTS

Instead of carrying the handgun on the vest, many entry teams carry their handguns in SAS-style drop holsters so that they are worn low on the thigh. Not only does this keep the handgun from interfering with the vest, but it makes it easier to reach when crouching, rappelling and so on. Many hostage rescue teams will have each member wearing a rappelling harness, belt, or vest fitted with Figure 8 descenders or carabiners so that he can quickly hitch himself for helicopter insertion or descent into a site. Whether built into the vest or separate, the Figure 8 Descender, a friction device for rappelling and belaying, and the Carabiner, an oval or 'D' shaped snap link used to connect ropes to an anchor point and descending devices to rappellers, are important items for any team which carries out insertions via rappel. Many teams supplement the other equipment with a rappelling sit harness with one or more built-in D rings. The choice of rappel rope is also important. Many hostage rescue teams consider Kernmantle rope the best choice. This rope incorporates nylon-fibre strands at the core surrounded by a loosely woven cover.

LADDERS

Teams will normally have available other aids to climbing, including an assortment of ladders. Some teams even have trucks with ladders hinged to the bed or roof so that the truck may quickly be driven next to a site, allowing the team to ascend quickly. Grappling hooks are also important.

GAS MASKS

As protection when gas or distraction devices are deployed virtually every hostage rescue team is equipped with gas masks. In the US, the most popular is probably the US military M17A1, which offers many useful features including three sizes, filters in the cheeks, ease of acquiring weapon sights through the lenses, compatible with prescription lenses for those with vision correction, protection against a wide range of agents and a carrier which allows a wide choice in where it is attached to the webbed gear or belt. The SF10 is widely used in the UK. This can fit an air tank which will enable the team member to swim if necessary.

ARMOURED VEHICLES

Depending on the team's budget, it might have specialised armoured vehicles for insertions, team vans with a myriad of equipment available, boats, diving gear and helicopters. Normally, the more sophisticated the equipment, the more time a team must devote to training. Although equipment is important, it is no more important than team selection and training.

EXAMPLE

Britain's Special Air Service offers a good object lesson. When the SAS was first given the counterterrorism mission, the Regiment had very little specialised equipment. It did, however, have highly trained men who were good at improvisation. Through experimentation and training – and eventually a lot of specialised equipment – the SAS became what many consider the world's premier hostage rescue unit.

CHAPTER 7

STEALTH OR SURREPTITIOUS VERSUS DYNAMIC ENTRY

Although stealth and dynamic entries have been mentioned in previous chapters it is important to make some additional points about the two types of entry.

It should be understood that surprise is the key element in both styles of entry. In the stealth or surreptitious entry the surprise is achieved through silence and camouflage, perhaps deception, to allow the rescue team to get very near the hostage-taker before he even realises they are there. The dynamic entry overwhelms and surprises the hostage-taker with its speed, noise and movement. In virtually all situations involving a stealth entry, a plan is in place to switch immediately to a dynamic entry if the entry is compromised, because once the hostages are in imminent danger, speed takes precedence over care in the approach, though safety of the entry team and the hostages still remains paramount.

STEALTH

TROJAN HORSE

One very effective type of stealth entry is what is often known as the 'Trojan Horse', the insertion of rescue personnel without the hostage-taker realising they are rescue personnel. UPS or other delivery trucks have been used, for example, to place a member of the rescue team at the door of a residence or office. Longer parcels, in fact, make excellent camouflage for a submachine gun. The 'Trojan Horse' has been used quite effectively on aircraft hijackings to insert members of the rescue team disguised as maintenance personnel or replacement flight crew. The SAS, in fact, has members of the unit train in flight simulators for the major airliners used by British Airways and other carriers so that, if necessary, they can pass as pilot or co-pilot and, at least, go through the preflight drills realistically. Many national hostage rescue units have trained pilots among their personnel, who, with simulator training, could at least begin to taxi the aircraft. More likely, however, is infiltrating rescue personnel as members of the service crew for an aircraft.

EXAMPLE

Perhaps the classic 'Trojan Horse' usage, though it was part of the deception plan as well as a method to insert personnel, occurred during the Israeli rescue at Entebbe. Using a Mercedes limo similar to that of Ida Amin and with a fake Amin, the Israelis approached the Ugandan troops helping to secure the airport by posing as the entourage and bodyguards for the dictator. So afraid of their leader were the guards that they froze for some time while the 'motorcade' approached, allowing the Israelis an advantage. Of course, once the shooting started, this rescue immediately became a dynamic one.

When carrying out a stealth or surreptitious approach to a hostage site, there are some basic premises which should be followed. First, have a plan and alternate route before even starting the approach. Bear in mind, also, two acronyms used by many US Army hostage rescue units.

The first is **BLISS**, five rules for effective camouflage during the approach.
- **B**lend with environment
- **L**ow silhouette
- **I**rregular shape
- **S**urvivability (i.e., have with you what you will need for the operation)
- **S**eclusion (i.e., approach from the most unexpected location)

COCOA is another useful acronym for basic rules of tactical movement.
- **C**over and Concealment
- **O**bservation
- **C**ritical Terrain
- **O**bstacles
- **A**venues of Approach and Escape

THE APPROACH

When moving towards the site, a team should move, halt, listen, observe, then move again. Slow precise movement allows members of the rescue team to approach as silently as possible. Watch ahead for obstacles which will create noise (i.e., twigs which can break, stones which might be kicked). Since noise is one of the most likely ways in which a stealth approach will be betrayed, great care must

Unless otherwise stated, all photographs appearing between pp. 113-128 are taken from the author's private collection.

Left A team member migrating across woodland during training. The site of the incident should be carefully evaluated when containing suspects or launching a rescue attempt; the assessment should include notes on potential obstacles or areas of concealment.

Below A US Army hostage rescue team practises infiltration to a site across a rooftop. An advantage of the roof entry is that it allows for stealthy insertion into a building by ladder, helicopter or adjoining building.

Hostage rescue personnel undergo a drill wearing gas masks. Gas has proven highly effective in forcing suspects to vacate a site, but also limits the vision of the entry team. Shooting while wearing gas masks is an important part of hostage rescue training.

Hostage teams may be inserted into a site in a multitude of ways, as this team from the Kennedy Space Center illustrates. This airboat is used to patrol the terrain around the center; adjunct members of the SWAT team help to keep intruders out! *(Kennedy Space Center)*

A member of a police entry team, and (right) a sniper from the same team. Communication between snipers and the entry team is essential when assaulting the site. Snipers may be called upon to cover the entry team during the approach, to direct them to their target or to observe and eliminate hidden suspects.

Members of the Special Air Service enter the Iranian Embassy from multiple points during the Princes Gate Assault of 30 April 1980, an incident which catapulted the SAS – and hostage rescue techniques – into the limelight. *(22nd SAS)*

Helicopter fast rope or rapel/abseil is often the fastest insertion method for a hostage rescue team. Kit is specifically customised to assist with this approach, and is likely to include harnesses, drop holsters, Figure 8 Descenders, and so on.

The 'SWAT Round-Up' competition in Memphis, TN puts evacuation techniques to the test. *(Dan Meany)*

A member of the Hungarian National Police Counter-terrorist unit practises rappelling during the 'SWAT Round-Up' competition. *(Dan Meany)*

Two US Army entry team members prepare to practise room clearing, armed with a Beretta M9 pistol (right) and a Heckler & Koch MP5 SMG.

A five-man entry team prepares for an assault. Note that the lead man is counting down with his fingers prior to entering the site. The number two man is armed with an Heckler & Koch MP-5.

Considered by many to be the world's best sniping rifle, the Accuracy International PM – L96A1 in British military designation – allows the majority of tactical marksmen to maximise their skills.

The author's Scattergun Technologies Remington 870 shotgun is choked so that it may be used for head shots in a hostage situation. A standard shotgun, however, will not normally be precise enough for such usage.

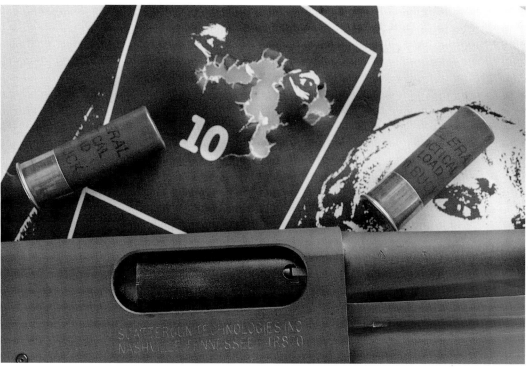

Members of hostage rescue units must train to shoot in situations where a shot will have to be fired very near to a hostage.

Snipers may have to take up a position using any available cover, in this case the bank of a lake. In urban areas, snipers may position themselves within 100-200 yards of their target.

As power is often cut prior to an entry, team members will usually have lights mounted onto their weapons.

The stun grenade is an invaluable distraction device for rescue teams. These were particularly successful during the terrorist attack against a Lufhansa jet at Mogidishu in October 1977. By drawing the terrorists to the front of the plane, GSG-9 freed all hostages on board.

Marksmanship skills are critical for those training in hostage rescue. The handgun pictured is a Glock 20 semi-auto pistol.

Realistic training scenarios are continually played out in facilities such as this tyre house. In this case, a 'terrorist' with his hand poised over the switch for an explosive device, and guarded by a fellow subject, must be eliminated with a head shot.

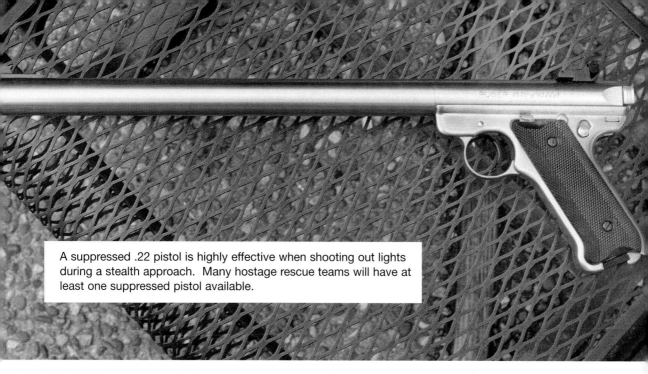

A suppressed .22 pistol is highly effective when shooting out lights during a stealth approach. Many hostage rescue teams will have at least one suppressed pistol available.

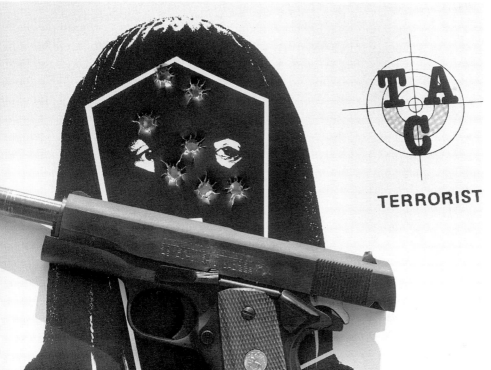

TERRORIST

With many US hostage rescue units, variations of the Colt Government Model .45 auto are a popular choice. Models are customised to attain enhanced sights, trigger pull and accuracy.

The Heckler & Koch MP5SD offers great versatility, both for situations where keeping the noise at a minimum is paramount, but also for scenarios where muzzle flash might present a problem, such as in a gas or chemical-filled environment.

37mm chemical munitions and the M-203 grenade launcher mounted on an AR-15 rifle.

The Robar QR2-F custom Remington 700 folding stock sniping rifle, which is compact yet highly precise. The sniping rifle is invaluable when the sniper has to infiltrate a location. The camouflage pattern is specifically designed for use within the urban environment.

The author instructing US Army personnel in bus assault techniques from the front. Of the men who initially enter the bus, at least one is assigned to either cover the driver from the front of the bus or from the driver's side window. The latter positon may also give him access to the door release.

A rescue team practises an assault from the rear of a bus. For the clearing team, the advantage in entering from the back is that they will be able to overlook each passenger seat as they approach and any shooter will have to turn to face them, increasing the latter's vulnerability. Two cover men are deployed to cover each side of the aisle, thus avoiding crossfire.

An external view of an assault on a public transit-style bus. In general, teams of between five and ten men are used. A minimum of four men are needed to actually board the bus, two to cover the passengers and two to move down the aisle checking for weapons and suspects.

For rescues at sea, personnel should train to 'wet jump' directly into a body of water. Divers and combat swimmers are highly-trained to adapt to murky water conditions when assaulting vessels or gathering intelligence during sea-based operations. *(National Archives)*

be taken to remain silent. Frequently, if an approach is compromised, it comes from a senior officer on the scene who is unfamiliar with rescue tactics and leaves on a radio or attempts to gain credit by approaching with the rescue team. One tactic which helps prevent the hostage-takers from hearing an approaching rescue team is raising the ambient noise level around the site.

EXAMPLE

During the Princes Gate siege in London, planes on approach to Heathrow Airport were actually lowered slightly by air traffic controllers to increase the noise level. In another case, when General Dozier was rescued from the Red Brigades, road construction equipment was used to increase the noise level. Ladders, hooks and other metal gear which will be used should be padded to deaden sound when they are emplaced on a wall, door, etc.

CONCEALMENT

Teams can also be compromised during an approach if they are seen. Carefully selecting cover or concealment points which allow the team member to blend with shadows is important. It is even possible to create shadows by selectively eliminating certain lights around a site or by moving around spotlights. By using a low or high crawl to stay near to the ground, the team member will hide his silhouette much more effectively. When there is no alternative to crossing open ground, such crawls can be combined with the rush from position to position, being exposed for no more than three to five seconds. When crossing open terrain another member of the team should cover the man carrying out the crossing. It is also important to have already selected the next cover before moving in open terrain. When using the rush, if the team member has fired his weapon, he should roll right or left before beginning the rush so an opponent will not know where to watch for him. If his position is concealed but not covered, then he should not fire at the hostage-takers because of the danger of drawing fire.

During the stealth approach, it is critical to watch the background at all times. A rescuer against a white wall will most likely stand out. Do not use lights; thus, on very dark nights or when moving through tunnels or some other entry points it may be necessary to use night vision goggles. (In urban areas utility service tunnels may allow an approach to near a building.) Brushing against objects both outside and inside the site can create noise. As a result, well-fitted clothing is important. Whenever possible blend with any obstructions which can be used as cover or concealment. Be especially aware that gun barrels or feet can protrude and give one away. This is especially true when at a corner of a building or on the interior at a hallway corner. As a result, it is better to 'slice the pie' or 'quarter' a corner (see Diagram 7.1). When peeking around a corner, first peek low, as anyone observing will most likely be looking at human-head height. Also, quick shots tend to go high so, combined with a subject's tendency to look high, this will be much safer if a shooter is encountered.

The 'Limited Entry'

During stealth entries, instead of full room entry techniques, a team may employ what are known as 'limited entry methods', in which team members attempt to take a quick look into a room while remaining ready to shoot, yet do not enter.

AUTHOR'S NOTE

One such method is termed the 'Israeli Limited Entry' and is based on the two entry men looking around the doorframe, exposing only their head and weapon arm. However, it should be noted that in many buildings in the US, the walls behind which the men are concealed do not really grant cover since a hostage-taker could shoot right through the wall beside the door. The technique was developed for use in Israel where walls are much more likely to have been constructed of blocks. The Israelis also use this technique because so many of the terrorists they encounter use grenades. The assumption is that one of the two shooters can take out the grenade thrower before he hurls it. Obviously, it is safer to remain outside the room in this scenario.

Camouflage

To blend in during an approach, especially at night, choose colours that blend with the grays and black of shadows. Specific urban camouflage patterns are available for such purposes. Watch also for glare from spit-shined boots, glasses, or other shiny objects. In addition to a jump test to check for noise before beginning the approach, do a quick glare inspection of each team member.

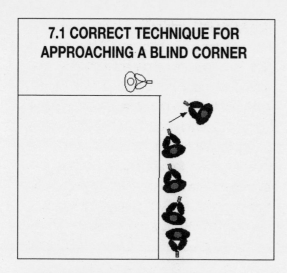

7.1 CORRECT TECHNIQUE FOR APPROACHING A BLIND CORNER

THE INTERIOR OF THE BUILDING

Once inside a building during a surreptitious entry, even more care must be taken to remain quiet and to avoid giving away the team's presence. For example, when moving, be aware that shadows can be visible beneath doors if they temporarily block the light. Buildings with carpets are much preferred to those with tile or wood floors, as the carpet will help deaden sound.

Bypassing Locks

It will be very likely that locks will have to be bypassed during surreptitious entry. First, check that doors are actually locked. They may not be. It is also likely,

particularly in business or industrial buildings, that it will be possible to locate someone who has keys. Generally, lock-picking is too time consuming, though members of national counterterrorist teams such as the FBI HRT, Delta, the SAS and GSG-9 will probably have received training in picking locks. Experienced entry teams have developed techniques for bypassing most types of locks. For example, knob door locks can usually be broken open by twisting them with channel lock pliers, but of course this will generate noise. In some cases at residences the doors are ignored and aluminium siding is pried off, leaving just insulation and wallboard for the team to pass through.

AUTHOR'S NOTE

It is also a rule of thumb based on the experience of many US SWAT teams, that rear doors are usually weaker than front doors on most homes.

Insertion From Above

If it is necessary to enter a multi-storey building from an upper floor, ladders may be used, but for taller buildings over a couple of storeys, fire equipment or a 'cherry picker' – a basket on a crane used by many utility companies – may be used for insertion. For use of such equipment, however, there must be a side of the building which the hostage-takers cannot observe. Teams may also be inserted directly onto the top of a building via a helicopter or may fast rope down onto the roof. However, if this method is to be used during a surreptitious entry, helicopters should have been flying around the building for some time so that one approaching does not arouse suspicion.

DYNAMIC

During any stealth entry there always remains the possibility that at any time the approach may be compromised. If the stealth team is already inside the building and close to their objective, they may switch over to a dynamic entry at the point at which they are compromised. However, standard operating procedure is to have a 'Go Team' ready to carry out a dynamic entry from the time the rescue unit arrives on the scene.

GO-TEAM TACTICS

Initially, their plan will be very simple and

based on little intelligence about the site, hostage-takers or hostages. Normally, the 'Go Team' will only be sent in if it appears that all or many hostages will be killed or injured if they do not assault immediately. As an incident progresses, the 'Go Team' develops a more sophisticated plan, yet remains ready for an immediate entry if events dictate it. One acronym based on the initials of the SAS sums up the tactics of a 'Go Team' if it is employed:

- **S**peed
- **A**ggressiveness
- **S**urprise

These same tactics are true of any dynamic assault where the basic mission is to gain control of the hostage-takers through surprise, firepower and speed.

Dynamic entry is usually considered to be justified in any of three circumstances:

1 Hostages are in imminent danger of being killed or injured.

2 A barricaded subject could endanger innocent people through his actions. (In one of the situations discussed earlier where an NBC threat is involved, this would be especially applicable.)

3 The subject will probably endanger police officers or other personnel through his hostile actions if not stopped.

Some general precepts for carrying out a dynamic entry include:

1 Use as many entry points as possible, but avoid situations where personnel might be caught in crossfire.

2 Try to enter where least expected.

3 Surround the site to cut off avenues of escape.

4 Hit fast, hard and with surprise.

5 Regroup before assaulting each room.

6 Keep good communication among members of the team.

7 Assign at least two men to clear each room.

8 Use distraction devices whenever possible.

9 Don't assume anyone is innocent (i.e., a terrorist could be posing as a hostage or the Stockholm Syndrome could have come into play).

TYPES OF DYNAMIC ENTRY

Generally, during a dynamic entry a 'swarm entry', in which as many personnel enter as possible to dominate a site, is desirable. Some teams employ four men for entries during dynamic entries and use variations of what is termed the 'Wall Flood' in which the first two men still clear the corners, but they are immediately followed by two more men to dominate the room completely (see Diagram 7.2). During a crisis-entry when speed is critical, these sets of two men may leapfrog each other, with the follow-on men becoming the first through the door of the next room. On the other hand, a 'snake entry', in which personnel enter in a line, may be more desirable during a stealth entry.

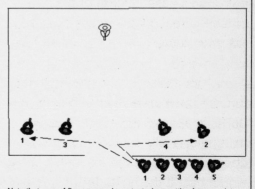

7.2 WALL FLOOD FOUR-MAN DYNAMIC ENTRY

Note that arcs of fire are very important when putting four men into a room quickly. Note also that Man #5 will continue to cover the hallway and the back of the four men carrying out the entry.

Dynamic entries must, of necessity, remain simple and must rely on surprise. Because the swarm entry may be used, a team must be very careful to avoid what is often termed the 'fatal funnel', in which personnel are so bunched that a terrorist or hostage-taker with an automatic weapon could wreak havoc on the entry team.

OVERCOMING BARRIERS

Often, windows will offer an appealing point of entry during either a dynamic or a stealth entry. While carrying out a stealth entry, attempts may be made to cut and remove glass to avoid noise. However, during a dynamic entry, glass may be broken out. In this case, shards of glass can present a real danger to members of the entry team.

Another aspect of a dynamic entry may be the explosive entry in which a portal is opened or a door is blown using a carefully selected explosive charge. Generally, the explosive entry works best if the hostage-taker is near the entry point. Once the entrance is blown, the team should be ready to

'Go! Go! Go!' to follow up any surprise gained from the sudden entry. Even after the entry point has been blown, it may be advisable to deploy distraction devices.

Both the dynamic and stealth or surreptitious entry have their place in entry tactics. The skilful hostage rescue team will have practised both and will have standard operating procedures in place for carrying out either type of entry. It may well be, in fact, that while one entry team is attempting a stealth approach and entry a second team is waiting to carry out a dynamic entry should the first team be discovered or in support of their entry. The stealth entry, for example, might have the mission of getting a team to the room where hostages are being held to allow them surgically to eliminate a hostage-taker assigned to guard them. Nearby, however, might be the bulk of the terrorists or hostage-takers, which might require a second team to carry out a dynamic entry to prevent them attacking the stealth team or attempting to harm the hostages.

Many of the basic tenets of building entries have been covered in previous chapters; however, in this chapter some additional special considerations will be discussed, as will entries in special circumstances and in certain types of buildings where hostage incidents might take place.

PLANNING ASSAULTS ON BUILDINGS

Since the largest number of hostage incidents take place within some type of building, hostage rescue teams train the most for building clearing operations. The great differences between carrying out a rescue at a school versus a trailer park make it extremely difficult to anticipate the exact circumstances which will confront a team carrying out a rescue. In fact, the best teams purposely build unanticipated problems into training scenarios. National hostage rescue teams and those protecting large urban areas often train at the sites where the possibility of a hostage incident might logically occur: for example, airports, courthouses, official residences, schools, prisons, nuclear facilities, national monuments, military facilities, banks and hotels.

VIDEO TAPING AND SURVEYS

Whenever possible, these training exercises are videotaped, both to allow critique and to build a library containing footage of potential sites of a rescue. Even when training is not carried out at such venues, teams will often video tape the interior and exterior, noting whether doors open inward or outward, types of locks and all the other information likely to be helpful if an incident takes place at the site. Close cooperation with the fire department can be invaluable in doing site surveys since fire marshals often carry out intensive surveys of all public buildings and often have extensive files of blue prints and notes on methods of gaining entry during an emergency.

AUTHOR'S NOTE

It is an interesting side note that in the US there are a few agencies in which safety personnel are trained as emergency medical technicians, police officers and firefighters, and alternate carrying out the different functions. Not only does this give the agency an extremely well-trained pool of personnel, but offers excellent potential for recruiting SWAT team members.

CHOOSING THE TYPE OF ENTRY

One of the first considerations in carrying out a building entry is choosing the specific type of entry: door entry, window entry, roof entry and rappel entry. For certain circumstances, the explosive entry through a wall or an entry through tunnels or ducts may also be considered.

Window Entry

The window entry, though often used as the second point of entry, has the disadvantage of being slower than a door entry and, thus, often results in a more lengthy exposure of the personnel carrying out the entry. Teams should acquire window frames and build a training wall where personnel can practise clearing windows while presenting the lowest profile possible.

Roof Entry

The advantage of the roof entry is that it allows for a relatively stealthy insertion by ladder, helicopter, cherry picker or from an adjoining building. Many teams prefer, too, to clear a building from the roof down since they feel that this will give hostage-takers less feeling of being trapped than if they are driven upwards towards the roof. It is also easier to carry out the clearing of stairways when moving down than moving up. Finally, hostage-takers or barricaded suspects may go ahead and surrender to containment personnel if they hear the SWAT team moving down from above. The rappel entry is usually carried out through windows after descending via a rope. France's GIGN practises rappel entries quite extensively as well as entries after free climbing up the side of a building. Many European shuttered windows lend themselves to the GIGN style entry whereby the rappeller swings outward and breaks through the window feet first, engaging any targets as he enters the room. This manoeuvre looks very impressive when demonstrated but takes intensive practice to perform competently as there is a danger of bouncing off the shutter on impact.

ENTRY POINTS

When planning an entry into a building, it is normally best to have at least two entry points. Generally, if the building is rectangular, it is better to enter at one end rather than the middle so that it is only necessary to clear in one direction. When carrying out the initial entry and, then, later when clearing rooms, personnel should avoid moving from a lighted area to a darkened area as they will be silhouetted while an enemy will not. If enough personnel are available, as each room is cleared someone should be left to secure it. However, this will often not be possible and the rear guard for an entry team will be required to find a point from which he can cover the doorways of multiple rooms which have already been cleared. Many teams carry wedges so that once a room has been cleared they can secure it externally so no one will be able to exit it. When clearing rooms, double doors will sometimes be encountered. In this case, it is normally better to open both doors when carrying out entry to allow maximum speed in clearing the doorway and to allow the best view of the room during the entry.

EXAMPLE

In a lengthy hostage incident, some real creativity may be used in choosing an entry point. During the assault on the Japanese ambassador's residence in Lima, for example, the Peruvian rescue team dug an extensive tunnel system to allow the team to emerge very close to the hostage-takers.

HELICOPTERS

Helicopters have been discussed for insertions, but they may also be used to aid entry in other ways. Although the media should be kept away from the site of an incident, media helicopters may be allowed to film at a distance what appear to be preparations for entry at a certain point, when in actuality, the real entry will come elsewhere. Such a diversion would normally only be used if intelligence indicated the hostage-taker was watching news reports and/or there was a particularly persistent media helicopter overhead. By having police helicopters flying around the site constantly, the hostage-taker will become accustomed to their presence and will be less likely to notice if they are used to insert a team on the roof. Police helicopters can also be used to raise the noise level to cover entry sounds or can use their high-powered searchlights (i.e., a Nightsun, which has 30 million candlepower) to blind or disorient a subject during an assault.

BATTERING RAM

Some teams have armoured cars which can be used with a ram to force entry through a particularly difficult door. These vehicles are also useful for retrieving wounded officers or hostages. Normally, teams which have such vehicles will have practised manoeuvres to use them as moving cover for an assault element which has to move over completely open ground. Specialised armoured vehicles can be useful to the hostage rescue effort, but just as the armoured vehicle on the battlefield needs infantry support, the SWAT armoured vehicle must be supported with trained entry personnel when carrying out a hostage rescue in a building.

Whether using an armoured vehicle as a ram or a using hand-held ram, one blow should take down the door or surprise will be lost. This is one reason that it is important to allow those personnel who will use the battering ram to practise on doors in condemned buildings or elsewhere. Experienced ram-men will learn to exert maximum force with minimum effort by using the ram as a pendulum. Even when other breaching methods are used – whether a ram or explosive breaching – it is advisable to have a member of the team armed with a shotgun loaded with Shok-Lok or other door-busting rounds in case unexpected locked doors are encountered.

RADIO COMMUNICATION PROCEDURES

Prior to carrying out an entry on a building or elsewhere, tactical radio communication procedures should be well established. Have 'procedure words' – known as 'prowords' – to shorten communications. For example, 'Authenticate', tells whoever is transmitting that they must respond to a challenge to establish their credibility. This response will normally be a short authentication code, perhaps a number or letter. Because gunfire can make it difficult to hear, many teams now use specialised earmuffs which amplify normal speech or other sounds but shut out the debilitating effects of gunfire. Such muffs designed for SWAT personnel allow the use of a radio earplug while being worn. During an entry commands should be short and unambiguous, both to other team members and to any suspects encountered. Those to suspects should be given in a confident, command voice. Such commands might include, 'Step into the open!' or 'Show me your empty hands!'

AUTHOR'S NOTE

Despite its popularity in films, 'Drop your weapon' is probably not a good command since the weapon might well go off when it hits the floor.

Probably more members of entry teams around the world have been shot by members of their own team who had accidental discharges from their weapons than by terrorists or criminals. As a result, it is important when doing entries for each man to carry weapons at the low ready so that the muzzle is not pointed at the man in front of him. However, some teams have concluded that there is a tendency for the muzzle to stray when carried in this position--a point which seems to be borne out by the number of entry team members

who have suffered gunshots to the thigh, calf or ankle during entries or entry training. Therefore, as an alternative, some teams train personnel to enter with their gun muzzles pointed upwards and positioned so that each man's muzzle is above the head of the man in front of him.

PRECISION OF MOVEMENT

Part of the danger of a firearms accidental discharge occurs when a team attempts to move too quickly during an entry. Other dangers from too rapid movement include not recognising a threat which presents itself or not being able to deal with it effectively. Although many teams train to clear rooms quickly, they normally use a fast walk rather than a run when moving into and through a room. Many train to shoot while advancing, keeping their balance forward so they present a good shooting platform while moving. It is, however, still better to shoot and move rather than attempting to shoot on the move. It is also possible when clearing some areas to assume a shooting position and move with a shuffling movement that retains the 'shooting platform' established by the legs and feet.

One specific area where precision of movement is paramount is when moving up a stairwell. When a four-man team is carrying out such movement, the first two men should cover straight ahead, the third man should cover up and the fourth man should cover down. Although it is not advised for two men to attempt to ascend a stairwell by themselves, there is a method in which they move slowly up the stairs back-to-back, with the front man covering forward and up and the rear man covering rearward and up.

SCHOOLS

Perhaps the incident hostage rescuers fear the most is one involving large numbers of children. The presence of large numbers of defenceless innocents can create an extremely appealing target for the terrorist or the deranged 'active shooter'.

EXAMPLE

When the Royal Dutch Marines faced the task of rescuing a large number of hostages on the Depunt Train, they also had to plan for a simultaneous rescue of school children being held by the same South Moluccan terrorist group. Fortunately, this rescue worked well, but the Israelis faced one of their greatest counterterrorism disasters when forced to carry out a rescue at the school at Ma'a lot (see Appendix 1).

EXAMPLE

In the US, the Littleton, Colorado 'active shooter' disaster brought home the vulnerability of many schools and the difficulty in providing a timely response to such incidents (see Appendix 1).

ACTIVE SHOOTER INCIDENTS IN SCHOOLS

Active shooter incidents such as that at Littleton normally involve one or more armed individuals with some type of grudge against society who erupt violently at a school, a post office, an office building, or some other venue where a large number of people are gathered. Although not strictly speaking a hostage incident, since the shooter is normally intent on killing as many people as possible, hostage-rescue personnel are faced with many of the same difficulties as in a hostage incident.

However, there is normally not time for negotiations and, often, the situation is similar to one in which a hostage has been killed early in an incident. A 'go team' must be sent in immediately.

Much thought has been given to dealing with such active shooter incidents, particularly at schools. As a result, the following priorities have been established:

1 **Containment of Suspects.** Despite the desire to help the injured, rescue personnel must first attempt to stop the shooters from killing more innocent people; hence containment is the top priority.

2 **Rescue of Victims or Hostages.** Once the suspects are contained, personnel can sweep through the building attempting to find those who are injured or hiding.

3 **Apprehension of Suspects.** Once steps have been taken to prevent the suspects from killing anyone else, then rescue personnel can attempt to apprehend them or, if necessary, kill them.

CONTAINING THE SHOOTER

In an active shooter incident, the entry team will always have to balance two factors when clearing a school – saving victims versus stopping the shooter. It may, in fact, be necessary for the initial entry team to bypass the wounded in an attempt to contain the shooters so that more are not wounded or killed. The decision, in effect, becomes the good of the many versus the good of the few. Normally, however, emergency medical or evacuation teams will follow closely behind the teams sweeping the building.

Entry teams will most likely encounter students or teachers hiding throughout the labyrinth of halls and rooms which comprise a large school. Care will have to be taken to insure these really are victims rather than shooters and that the team is not trigger-happy. Because clearing a multi-storey school with dozens of hallways and hundreds of rooms can be so overwhelming, the entry teams may want to use coded wall markings to inform follow-up teams what areas have been secured and/or where other teams are.

WORKING WITH COMMUNITY RELATIONS OFFICERS

Because schools are governed by very strict fire codes and are constantly monitored by the fire department, plans of the school should be readily available form the fire department. Even more helpful is the fact that fire codes often require that floor plans with evacuation routes be placed in every school hallway or room. The problem with an active shooter incident, however, is getting the plans there on time. In the US, school community relations officers who are assigned to the school can be invaluable in assisting the entry team. They are usually armed, have an office at the school and may work with local SWAT personnel to create contingency plans for possible terrorist incidents. They will know where to go for photographs of the shooter or shooters if they are students or former students. They may also have a videotape of the school if they've previously done an emergency site survey. In many US schools, the public address systems are two-way and may be used to listen in to rooms around the building. If this is the case, intelligence can be gained about the whereabouts of the shooters or hostage-takers in this manner.

CHECKING THE BUILDING

In many schools, the plan for dealing with an active shooter incident is for students to be locked down in rooms with their teachers. Since schools are normally constructed with heavy masonry or block walls and heavy fire doors, such a plan can grant a degree of safety. However, entry teams will then be confronted with halls full of closed and locked doors without knowing which might hide a shooter. This is a case where an astute school administration or community relations officer could be invaluable in assisting teachers with methods of passing information to the search/entry team. Each teacher should for example have some method of quickly showing a team checking hallways that the room is secure. A brightly coloured computer mouse pad, for example, that could be slipped under the door, could help rescue personnel determine rooms that were secure. Obviously, the danger of duress would still exist and these rooms could not be considered fully secured until checked, but this could still speed up the search for shooters within a building.

The thick walls in schools have already been mentioned. This should give the entry team reasonable cover as they move through the building and also give a certain amount of 'backstop' for pistol calibre ammunition to prevent over penetration. Another consideration in schools is that many have sophisticated smoke detectors, which when set off immediately release all hallway doors from magnetic hold opens to present fire barriers. As a result, if distraction devices or gas is employed, the entry team must realise they will be slowed considerably in moving through the building because in each hallway they will encounter these heavy doors which have automatically closed.

TRAINING IN SCHOOLS

Because of the design of schools with so many points of entry and egress, containment will also present a problem and will require a substantial number of personnel. Additionally, entry teams must be able to remain calm when confronted with potentially hysterical, perhaps injured children, in large numbers. Because virtually every community has a school or schools within their boundaries, any hostage rescue unit should attempt to train at their schools to learn the specialised characteristics of each building. Any preplanning and pre-

knowledge can be invaluable should the school become the scene of a hostage or active shooter incident.

CORRECTIONAL FACILITIES

THE INMATE POPULATION

Hostage situations at prisons can become especially dangerous due to the nature of the inmate population. In a prison incident, it is a given that the hostage-takers will most likely be dangerous individuals, quite possibly convicted murderers or violent criminals. As hostage incidents in prisons often evolve into situations in which the prisoners take revenge on guards or other prisoners, it may be necessary to have an assault plan in place quickly. In fact, assault plans should already be in plan for any correctional facility whether it is one covered by the Federal Bureau of Prisons SERT (Special Emergency Response Team), by state police SWAT, or by national counterterrorist teams such as GIGN which has handled many prison incidents in France. Even more important than in most hostage situations, in incidents at correctional facilities, the negotiator must have the threat of a quick and deadly armed response available should the hostage-takers begin harming hostages.

CLEARING A CORRECTIONAL FACILITY

There are certain pluses and minuses which are inherent in hostage incidents at a prison. Because correctional facilities are designed to keep inmates inside and others out, it is generally easy to set up containment for a prison incident, even one involving a large number of inmates. Because of the large number of surveillance cameras in most modern prisons, theoretically, intelligence should be easily gained; however, in a riot, it is quite likely that the cameras will be broken very quickly.

Because prisons are designed as hardened facilities, getting into them through breaching can often present problems. The walls are very thick and doors are constructed of steel. In some instances a large variety of electronic and mechanical locks will be in place for opening and closing doors. Knowing which ones control access to different areas is extremely critical to any team attempting to clear a correctional facility. In fact, because of the specialised design of correctional facilities, it is best if a trained hostage-rescue team drawn from corrections officers is available. If not, corrections officers should work closely with the team which will be doing the entry to apprise them of any useful information.

Body Armour

A team carrying out operations in a correctional facility may also have to give some specialised consideration to their body armour. Normally, SWAT body armour is chosen to stop bullets. However, it is entirely possible that in clearing a prison, teams will encounter subjects armed with 'shanks', makeshift knives. The normal SWAT glove or BDU covering arms will give little protection against blades; thus, consideration should be given to specialised gauntlets.

USING FORCE

Because of the violent nature of those likely to be encountered in clearing a correctional facility, rules of engagement should be set which grant personnel clear authority to use deadly force if resistance is met, and great care must be taken in arresting those subjects who surrender. Bear in mind that, quite often, they will have spent many hours in prison practicing techniques of turning on an officer attempting to frisk or handcuff them.

Since prisons are usually designed with sniping towers, these might offer a possibility for a team's tactical marksman. However, the towers are usually designed to cover open areas of the prison such as the exercise yard or approaches to gates and walls. Therefore, it is probable that tactical marksmen will have to infiltrate to other positions within the prison complex which give them a view of the area occupied by the hostage-takers. Correctional facility design is such, however, that finding a good sniper/observer position may not be possible. Generally, prison incidents, if not solved through negotiation, have to be solved by entry teams which work their way through the facility.

Chemical Agents

Chemical agents are always a possibility at correctional facilities; however, there may be special circumstances that hinder their use. At least some prisons, for example, have what is known as 'positive airflow' in cell blocks, which can make gas far less effective. Some prisons also have 'dead spots' where gas will not penetrate in sufficient quantity to take effect. A cell block designed in the shape of a 'U', for example, would probably allow hostage-takers to retreat to the curve if the chemical agents were introduced at either or both ends of the block.

INTELLIGENCE

Once again it should be emphasised that because of the complex organisation and design of prisons, plans should already be in place for dealing with hostage incidents and video tapes and plans, preferably computer generated, should be in place to assist those who will have to clear the correctional facility. It is highly desirable, too, to have a team drawn from personnel who know the correctional facility, the potential hostages and the potential hostage-takers.

NUCLEAR FACILITIES

When planning for a potential hostage incident at a nuclear facility, some very specialised considerations apply. First, as has already been discussed in Chapter 5 on barricaded suspects, at a nuclear facility, an entire community or city may be considered the hostages. As a result, the team must be ready to make the choice of the lives of a couple of hostages held in the facility versus the integrity of the facility. If such a choice arises, the integrity of the facility is paramount. Fortunately, most nuclear facilities are so designed that getting to the critical areas is extremely difficult.

FIRE AND MANOEUVRE

It should also be assumed that an incident at a nuclear facility will be engendered by terrorists or other heavily armed individuals since they will have got past a well-trained and well-armed security force. As a result, nuclear response teams tend to practise approaches which are akin to military small unit tactics involving fire and manoeuvre. Normally, part of each team will assume an 'overwatch' mode while the rest of the team moves. It is also more likely that members of a nuclear response team will be armed with rifle-calibre weapons due to the threat they will probably encounter, though they may have submachine guns with highly frangible ammunition for use in certain areas of the facility. Should the use of firearms seem inappropriate to the reader, it is important to note that the most sensitive areas of a nuclear plant are usually contained within a highly bullet and fire resistant realm. In addition, nuclear response teams would have been thoroughly briefed regarding the locations in which they are able to shoot if necessary, and those requiring them to hold fire.

Once again, though national counterterrorist units may have some responsibility at nuclear facilities, it is best if a nuclear facility response team is drawn from the facility's security force and especially trained for operations in the nuclear environment, including use of HazMat suits if necessary.

Computers have been a real boon to hostage rescue teams having to operate in various types of buildings. Not only do computers allow plans to be quickly located, but copies can be run for team members and diagrams detailing entry plans can be quickly generated. In assaulting buildings, practice on an apartment, office, or complex as close to the one to be assaulted is highly desirable. Multiple entry points and alternative entry plans are also highly critical. As stated before, hostage rescue teams should cultivate commercial real estate firms and construction companies that specialise in demolishing buildings. They should also work with security personnel at courthouses, hospitals and so on to allow training in these facilities. The more hallways and stairways on which a team has practised the more confident they will be when they have to clear a building for real and the more likely they will have been to have encountered potential delays and learned how to deal with them.

The best advice in training for building entries is, find buildings on which to train for building entries!

CHAPTER 9

OPERATIONS AGAINST VEHICLES AND TRAINS

Normally, the premise in counter-terrorist or hostage-rescue operations is to keep the incident contained and prevent it from 'going mobile'. In the case of a train hijacking, the incident will normally take place when the train is either already en route or awaiting departure. This is a separate situation which will be discussed later in the chapter. Incidents involving automobiles, however, can originate as a mobile situation – a car jacking, for example – or can occur when a hostage-taker requests a vehicle to be provided.

Buses are also targets for hijackings or may have been provided to the hostage-takers if a large number of hostages and/or hostage-takers are involved. Once again, tactics for assaulting automobiles or buses once a hostage incident is taking place in them will be discussed later.

CONSIDERATIONS WHEN SUPPLYING TRANSPORT

First, however, it is important to understand the considerations faced by an incident commander when hostage-takers ask for transport to be provided. The primary element in making this decision is whether allowing the hostage-taker transport will make it easier or harder to rescue the hostages. If, for example, the hostage-taker is in a building that will be almost impossible to assault successfully, then allowing him to go mobile might be a viable option. Another possibility is that in choosing to go mobile, the hostage-takers will not be able to take all of the hostages and will, thus, release some of them. For example, if two hostage-takers are holding ten hostages and ask for a standard passenger car, then it can be assumed that seven or eight of the hostages will be released. The incident commander may choose to play the odds and gain their release. The hostage negotiator can work out the details.

THE SNIPER OPTION

If the hostage-taker is going to move a hostage or hostages to a vehicle, then the possibility of either ending the situation with a shot from one of the snipers or of assaulting while the movement is in progress must be considered. Even if the sniper option is chosen, an assault team should be ready to follow-up. It should be borne in mind, however, that the hostage-taker will be particularly watchful during this move. As a result, some teams use tactics to make it easier to eliminate the hostage-taker. For example, the automobile could be pulled up in front of the building, turned off and the keys placed on the roof of the driver's side. This might result in a shot for the sniper when the hostage-taker reaches for the keys. Another ploy might be to park the vehicle so that the snipers have a shot into the vehicle from either front or back as the hostage-taker enters it.

SUPPLYING A PRE-PREPARED VEHICLE

Still other tactics are based on supplying a vehicle which is pre-prepared for an assault.

If asked to supply a vehicle, some teams have five rules for that vehicle:

1 The windows should be rolled down and locked there.

2 Door looks should be inoperable.

3 Mirrors should be removed.

4 The engine should be capable of remote cut-off.

5 Remotely operated distraction devices or chemical munitions should be installed in the vehicle.

The disabled windows and door locks on the prepared vehicle allow rapid entry for an assault team. The lack of mirrors makes it easier for an assault team to approach the vehicle undetected. The remote engine cut-off allows the vehicle to be stopped at the best position for an assault.

Some agencies have remote engine cutoffs available which can be installed in as little as a minute and, which, with proper practice on the part of the operator, can bring a vehicle to a stop where an assault team is waiting with surprising precision. Other methods, such as supplying a vehicle with only a small amount of gasoline, are much less precise.

ASSAULTING A COVERED PILE

One situation which may arise when a hostage-taker is removing a hostage to a vehicle is what some agencies term the 'covered pile'. In this gambit, the hostage-taker covers the hostage and himself with a blanket to prevent snipers from taking a shot. At least some teams, however, practise an assault based on the use of the covered pile.

One technique for dealing with the 'covered pile' requires a five-man assault team which approaches from the rear. In this technique, two of the team members quietly approach and grab the edges of the blanket, jerking it upward and away from the hostage and hostage-taker. Based on the assumption that most shooters will be right-handed, another team member, often one with a martial arts background, will move in from the right to immobilise the hostage-taker's weapon's hand and arm. The fourth team member, armed with a handgun, comes in from the left and, if necessary, eliminates the hostage-taker at point blank range. The final member of the team grabs the hostage and takes him or her to the ground for safety (see Diagram 9.1).

ASSAULTING AN AUTOMOBILE

If it is necessary to assault an automobile to rescue a hostage there are some basic premises which have proved successful.

STOPPING THE VEHICLE
First, the vehicle has to be stationary. The ability to cut the engine remotely has already been discussed. Although shooting out the tyres has been used, this can cause an accident endangering the hostage and it is also debatable where the vehicle will stop.

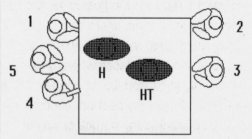

9.1 ASSAULTING A 'COVERED PILE'

If a hostage-taker attempts to remove a hostage from a site by placing a blanket over the heads of the hostage and the hostage-taker, then this is one type of assault which may be employed. Team members 1 and 2 grab the edges of the blanket and jerk it up and away from the hostage (H) and hostage-taker (HT). Team member 3 attempts to disable the hostage-taker's shooting arm, while team member 4 moves in for a point blank shot if necessary. Team member 5 grabs the hostage and takes him or her to the ground for safety.

9.2 TECHNIQUE FOR BLOCKING A MOBILE VEHICLE CONTAINING A HOSTAGE

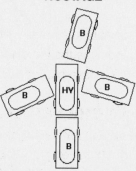

Note that the vehicle containing the hostage and hostage-taker (HV) is completely blocked by the four vehicles (B) designated to stop the vehicle. It cannot move forward or backward, nor can the hostage-taker or hostage-takers exit the doors of the vehicle. This contains the situation so that the rescue team can move in and take appropriate action.

The 'stop strips' which can be dragged across the road to stop fleeing vehicles offer a more effective alternative but can still be problematical. Some teams plan assaults based on places where a vehicle will be forced to stop (i.e., a bridge entrance), but it may be more effective to plan on a block using a truck or some other vehicle. It is best if the stop can be arranged just before a rise or when there is concealment or cover for the assault team nearby. Often, however, it will be necessary to carry out a forced stop. In this situation, it is best if the vehicle is blocked from advancing or retreating and if the doors or blocked so the hostage-taker cannot exit the car (see Diagram 9.2).

ASSAULTING THE VEHICLE

Once the vehicle has been stopped, the team will have to move quickly to get into position before the hostage-taker can harm the hostage. If snipers have been emplaced near the point of the vehicle stop, they may be in position to take a quick shot to end the situation. Certainly, they should give the assault team intelligence about the location of hostage-takers and hostages. The assault is usually carried out by at least six team members: four for the actual assault and two in support to break into the vehicle or extract subjects or hostages (see Diagrams 9.3, 9.4 and 9.5). It should be noted that hostage-takers should always be extracted from the vehicle or eliminated before attempting to extract hostages.

Because of the difficulty in breaking automobile safety glass, support men should have 'rake and break' tools such as the 'Hooligan Tool', which allow glass to be broken then quickly raked clear, but may also rely on spring-loaded punches.

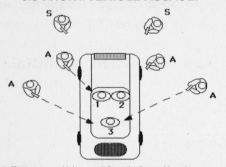

9.3 FRONT VEHICLE ASSAULT

This illustrates a vehicle assault from the front with a six-man team. Some rescue units prefer to use an eight-man team for vehicle assaults. With the six-man team, four members (A) act as the actual assault element, while two members act as the support element (S). Those assigned to support will deploy distraction devices or use tools to break the car glass or force the doors open. In this example, passengers 1 and 3 are hostage-takers and passenger 2 is the hostage.

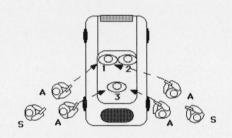

9.4 REAR VEHICLE ASSAULT

The rear assault is better suited for situations requiring the support element to breach the vehicle to extract the hostages or hostage-takers. Members of the assault element still cover all hostage-takers and are prepared to engage them upon the sign of any hostile action.

At least some teams have mounted punches at the muzzles of their H&K MP-5s so that they can break a window and immediately cover a suspect.

AUTHOR'S NOTE

Whichever type of punch is used, it is best to hit windows on the edge rather than in the centre.

ELIMINATING THE SUSPECT

In taking a shot at a hostage-taker within a vehicle, there can be many difficulties. Windows can be tinted, for example, requiring any shot to be taken from the front, though there are some sophisticated sighting devices which will allow a shot through tinted glass. A hostage-taker may also be located between two hostages, making a side shot virtually impossible. The FBI HRT used to practise an assault in which a team member ran onto the roof of the vehicle and took a shot directly down through the roof with a shotgun slug to eliminate the hostage-taker. In certain situations, this can be highly effective, but the location of the hostage-taker must be determined with a high degree of accuracy.

9.5 SIDE VEHICLE ASSAULT

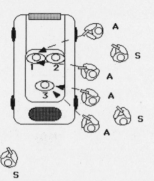

The side or column assault is used when one side of the vehicle is blocked by terrain or buildings. If it is necessary to extract hostage-takers or hostages from the vehicle it is done from the assault side. Note that an additional team member in support is added for this type of assault to cover the non-assault side.

When approaching a vehicle, members of the assault team must also make sure that they do not allow themselves to assume a position where they put themselves in danger of crossfire.

ASSAULTING A BUS

A hostage incident may occur on a public transit bus, a school bus or on a long-haul bus such as those used by Greyhound. Buses used to transport passengers between airport terminals or those shuttling prisoners to court might also be the scene of a hostage incident. Because there are so many potential hostage situations which might arise on a bus, many rescue teams practise assiduously on bus assaults.

EXAMPLE

Perhaps the most famous incident was the GIGN combination of precision sniper fire and assault upon a hijacked bus in Djibouti (see Appendix 1). Many other incidents, however, have occurred including recent ones in Korea and Brazil.

SUPPLYING A BUS

Bus incidents may arise as at the Munich Olympics when the authorities were asked to provide transport to the airport (see Appendix 1). Should the incident commander decide that providing a bus is desirable, certain considerations should be borne in mind. First, the type of bus supplied should be one which is common enough to allow a rescue team easily to acquire one upon which to practise assaults. It should also be one which allows the easiest entry and one which does not have tinted windows, which will inhibit the ability of snipers to gain intelligence or take a shot.

AUTHOR'S NOTE

Before supplying the bus, the driver's side mirror should either be broken (it can be claimed an inexperienced driver scraped a light post, etc. delivering the bus) or the mirrors should be adjusted to leave dead zones on the sides of the bus to allow an assault team to approach.

IMMOBILISING THE BUS

When planning a bus assault, coordination is paramount between snipers, assault teams, forced entry teams, blockers and distraction teams. If the bus is mobile, then one of the first considerations is getting it stopped. Possible stop points include red lights, sharp curves or just before the crest of a hill. If the stop is to be made at an urban intersection, then members of the assault team may want to be nearby dressed as passersby. A block vehicle may be used to immobilise the bus, but it must be large enough to block a bus effectively. The assault team may have to be in a van trailing the bus, ready to go into action as soon as the stop is made.

There are some more subtle ways to stop a bus. Most large public service buses, for example, have a remote switch located near the engine to start or stop the bus so that mechanics can test the engine while working on it. If possible, consult a mechanic familiar with the type of bus involved in the incident for information about remote shut down. Buses may also be disabled by cutting the brake lines or electrical lines. Normally, when the hydraulic brake line is cut, rear brakes lock bringing the bus to a stop or keeping it stationary. Getting a team member under a bus at a red light to cut the brake lines offers one possibility for rendering a bus immobile. Obviously, the team must have a cutting tool which has been pre-tested as strong enough to do the job quickly. It is important to have the assault team ready to follow up immediately once the vehicle is immobilised, to take full advantage of the disorientation within the vehicle caused by the surprise stop.

GAINING ENTRY

Once the bus has been immobilised, the next important step is gaining entry. On most buses, door controls are located just inside the driver's window, a window which is normally not locked (to allow access when the driver leaves the bus). On public service type buses, the front door is operated hydraulically and the rear door is operated electronically. Since hydraulic lines may be cut in stopping a bus, it is important to know if this will prevent the door being opened or will require greater force to be exerted on the door. Normally, as a backup, a team member should be equipped with a ram to take out the front door of the bus if necessary. On school buses, the rear door normally swings outward and is opened by turning a handle. It is important to check with the bus company whether or not this handle can be operated from outside the bus if a rear entry is contemplated. If it is locked but there is an external handle, it may be quickly forced open with heavy pliers.

LIMITING THE HOSTAGE-TAKER'S VISIBILITY

One problem in planning an assault on a bus is that the large number of windows normally gives a hostage-taker 360 degree visibility. As a result, a sniper may well be the best way to end a hostage incident aboard a bus if there is only one hostage-taker. If enough snipers are available to assign two to each hostage-taker and multiple hostage-takers are all in the crosshairs simultaneously, then snipers may also end an incident with multiple targets. If the bus has tinted windows, the sniper's job is much more difficult. Some hostage-takers may also paste paper over the windows or have passengers stand in front of windows to make a shot difficult. Such actions, of course, limit the hostage-taker's visibility and make it easier for the assault team to approach.

DISTRACTION DEVICES

Prior to an actual assault, distraction devices are generally more effective if thrown outside on the side of the bus away from the assault to attract attention. They may also be used outside of the vehicle. If used aboard a bus it should be remembered that, because of the contained space and the likelihood of the devices rolling under a seat, they may be dangerous if small children or those with medical problems are on board, or may be less effective than usual because the seat will screen their effects from the hostage-taker. Sometimes chemical munitions may actually be deployed from under the bus where the ventilation system is located.

ASSAULT TECHNIQUES

Various assault techniques have been used against buses, normally using teams of between five and ten men (see Diagrams 9.6 and 9.7). In general, at least four men are needed to actually board the bus, two to cover the passengers and two to move down the aisle checking for weapons and/or hostage-takers. If the hostage-takers have been previously identified and can be recognised, this task is much easier; however, all passengers should still be handcuffed and removed to be sure none was an accomplice. The fewer passengers on board the bus the better. Bear in mind, however, that a normal school bus will hold 65 children, so there may be a large number of hostages.

Initial Entry

The four men who initially enter the bus should quickly check low to make sure no gunmen are hiding beneath the seats before anyone begins moving down the aisles.   The first man on should yell very distinctly, 'Police (or FBI or SAS, etc.), hands up!' It may also be necessary to remove the driver and/or passengers in the front seats to allow the cover men a field of fire. Two cover men are best so that one

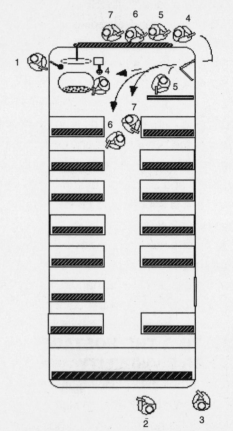

9.6 ASSAULTING A PUBLIC TRANSIT STYLE BUS

When assaulting a public transit type of bus, the minium needed is five men, though seven or eight is optimum. Team member #1 covers the driver and works the front door release. #2 prepares to cut the engine's power, while #3 gives rear cover. Note that he can also cover the rear exit. #4 and #5 enter, and immediately cover the passengers. It may be necessary for them to evacuate the driver and passengers in the front two seats. #6 and #7 will be in their shooting stances prepared to move down the aisle quickly checking each passenger. A detention team to remove passengers will follow.

9.7 ASSAULTING A SCHOOL BUS

Although this type of assault is often practised with eight men, it works best with a nine-man team. Team member #1 controls the driver and releases the front door. #2 and #3 act as bases to support #4 and #5 on their knees so they may peek into the rear of the bus by the rear door. If necessary they can take a shot on hostage-takers or begin an entry through the rear door. If the rear entry is carried out, #4 and #5 control the bus, while #2 and #3 enter to clear the bus. As an alternative, an entry similar to that used on public transit buses may be carried out through the front door.

can cover each side of the aisle and avoid crossfire. Submachine guns usually make the best armament for the cover men, though in this situation all but skilled users might want to set them on semi-automatic.

Clearing Passengers

There are two primary methods of clearing the passengers. In one, the clearing men quickly go through the bus to check for weapons, usually after ordering subjects to place their open hands on their heads. Then, an arrest team comes on and removes passengers one seat at a time after cuffing them with flex cuffs (until all hostage-takers/accomplices have been identified). If there are only a limited number of passengers, some like to follow up the team clearing with an arrest team which removes passengers as soon as the clearing team has checked that seat. This, however, puts too many people in the aisle should shooting start and makes it more difficult for the cover men to protect those checking the passengers.

The Cover Men

One man is usually assigned to either cover the driver from the front of the bus or from the driver's side window. The latter is preferable since he can also release the door. Some teams have cover men approach the bus from the sides and stand on a box or short ladder to cover the bus through side windows. Normally, however, if the two cover men get aboard the bus quickly they can do a more effective job because they are looking down the length of the bus, while cover men approaching from the side would have to use their peripheral vision too much. Still another option with a school bus having a rear door is to enter from the rear. Some teams put two cover men on board in this manner, while others have the clearing team move from the rear since they will be able to overlook each passenger seat as they approach and any shooter would have to waste time turning to engage them.

AUTHOR'S NOTE

In the author's experience, it is best for a rescue team to practise variations on the bus assault, then decide which one appears most effective for the team. Bear in mind, though, that each type of bus may require a slightly different type of assault. As a result, teams should arrange to practise on as many different types of buses as possible.

Whichever method is decided upon, it is important that:

- it does not put members of the assault or support teams in danger of crossfire,

- it deals with entry through at least one door; and

- it quickly puts at least two men to cover the bus on board.

Remember, too, that this is one type of incident where solution by use of snipers is often the most desirable.

EXAMPLE

A recent incident in Brazil offers the perfect example of how a sniper should have been employed. The single hostage-taker frequently came to an open window on the bus while holding a revolver to a hostage's head. However, he would then take the weapon away offering a perfect shot. Instead, the police tried to rush him as he left the bus with a hostage, missing him and killing the pregnant female hostage.

Since the shot may be through glass and possibly at an angle, however, at least two snipers must be assigned to each hostile subject.

ASSAULTING A TRAIN

Hostage incidents on board trains offer some marked advantages and disadvantages to a rescue team. Because trains are limited to travelling on their tracks, such incidents are often relatively easy to contain. In fact, it may be possible, if the engine is not under the control of the hostage-takers, to shuttle the train to a siding or a point in a railroad yard which offers good cover and concealment for a rescue team. Unless the train is stationary, an assault will be very difficult. On the negative side, an incident on board a train will normally involve a substantial number of hostages.

ENTERING THE TRAIN

Because of the linear nature of a train, whether of the light rail type or of the inter-city type, it takes a substantial number of hostage-takers to control multiple cars. If, however, there are more than one or two hostage-takers with hostages in multiple cars, then a rescue will require numerous assault teams. The linear nature of a train also will normally necessitate an entry from one end with clearing teams moving the length of the train. If entries are carried out from both ends of the train, unless a large number of cars are involved, then the chances of members of the assault teams accidentally shooting each other increase dramatically. Should the train be long enough that multiple entry points are indicated, then an assault plan which prevents members of the assault from force from becoming involved in a fire fight with 'friendlies' is extremely important. For example, if five cars are being cleared, the plan might call for one team to enter the rear car and clear it and the next one up the line, another team to enter the furthest forward car and clear it and the one behind it, while a third team enters the middle car and clears it.

USING MULTIPLE SHOOTERS

Ideally, hostage-takers on board a train would be eliminated without actually having to carry out an entry. If possible, snipers should be assigned to eliminate the hostage-taker or hostage-takers. Use as many snipers as possible to put multiple shooters on each subject. When considering snipers, however, bear in mind that many trains, particularly those such as 'Bullet Trains' or the Channel Tunnel train which travel very fast, will have specially hardened windows, especially in the engine. As a result, a sniper needs to know what type of glass through which he may have to take a shot. If an assault is necessary, however, it may be possible for members of the assault team to infiltrate close to the train, then eliminate the hostage-takers with a shot through the body of the train using penetrative ammunition or through a gun port created with an explosive cutting charge. Such a shooting port might be created at an unexpected point such as through the roof. Even if a sniper or a shot outside the compartment from an assault team member is contemplated, however, an assault team must be ready for immediate entry in case the hostage-takers cannot all be located or a shot is missed.

Gathering Intelligence

Since many railroad cars are equipped with shades which may be closed, snipers and observers may encounter some difficulty gathering intelligence. However, the nature of most rail beds, which are usually raised, allows the infiltration of team members to carry out recces or to emplace listening or video intelligence gathering devices.

PRACTICAL EXPERIENCE

If the incident lasts long enough, members of the assault teams should practise on a car of exactly the same layout as those which will be assaulted to rescue hostages. Special characteristics of the doors and windows should be noted as should blind spots which allow an approach along the side or under the car. Some US commuter trains have two levels which necessitate detailing two teams to clear those types of cars. During an assault, team members will need to be detailed to cover each side of the train to prevent a hostage-taker from exiting one car and entering another. It should be emphasised again that extreme care must be taken to avoid putting team members in danger of crossfire. Because of the linear nature of the train, a good plan will probably have a follow-up team moving in as soon as an assault team clears a car to quickly evacuate and secure hostages from that car.

DISTRACTION DEVICES

Trains which are compartmentalised will normally severely limit the effectiveness of distraction devices unless the hostage-taker is in the compartment into which the device is thrown. Devices of the 'Thunder Strip' type which are designed to be slipped beneath a door can be invaluable, however, if the hostage-taker is known to be in one compartment. In fact, the 'strip' can be detonated, while either an entry or a shot is effected through the window. Other external distractions which draw the attention of the hostage-taker can be useful. A fast train on a nearby track with whistles blasting might make an excellent distraction as would other activity around a railroad yard.

EXAMPLE

When the Royal Dutch Marines assaulted the Depunt Train, they felt it was important to cause both hostages and hostage-takers to keep their heads down while they were assaulting, so they had Royal Dutch Air Force jets fly low and kick in their afterburners.

As with assaults on other types of ground transport, successful train assaults are dependent on immobilizing the train at the most advantageous position possible. If the situation can be ended by a sniper, then this is to be preferred; however, a plan must be in place for an assault if the sniper fails. In a train, and to a lesser extent in a bus or automobile, knowing where the hostage-takers are located is of supreme importance. The availability of a weapon and/or ammunition which will allow a shot through the body of the vehicle or train may also be critical in successfully ending the incident. It should not be forgotten either that trains particularly, but other vehicles as well, must be checked carefully for explosive devices designed to either impede an entry or to allow a terrorist to destroy the train or vehicle. Most of all, assaults on vehicles or trains can be carried out most effectively if they have been practised in advance.

Rescue team training time should be devoted to scenarios involving hostage incidents involving automobiles, buses and trains. The team should also practise on as many different types of vehicle or train as possible.

CHAPTER 10

OPERATIONS AGAINST SHIPS AND AIRCRAFT

Hostage incidents aboard ships or aircraft give the hostage-taker far more control of the environment than do those at fixed sites. The fact that the incident occurs aboard a technically complex means of transport which carries the potential for massive loss of life if the ship sinks or the aircraft crashes puts far more constraints on a rescue team than do operations involving normal sites.

Ship or aircraft incidents also contain the potential for occurring all over the globe and of moving from point to point, both characteristics which can frustrate those tasked with rescuing hostages. Terrorists who hijack aircraft have, in fact, shown a good learning curve since the rescues at Mogidishu and Entebbe (see Appendix 1). Now, terrorists have much more of a tendency to keep the aircraft moving from airport to airport or to remove hostages and take them elsewhere. Because of the intensive training and specialised equipment necessary to carry out a rescue aboard a ship or aircraft, normally only the most sophisticated national counterterrorist units will have this capability.

ASSAULTING A SHIP

INTELLIGENCE

If an attempt is to be made at rescuing hostages held aboard a ship, a great deal of intelligence is needed. For example, there will be far different considerations if the target vehicle is a cruise ship, perhaps with thousands of passengers on board, than if it is a giant super tanker with only a small crew but potential for environmental disaster.

Among the information which can prove particularly useful is that related to the interior:
- passageways,
- hatches,
- stairways,
- construction of bulkheads (steel, aluminum, other materials?),
- how hatches and portholes open,
- access routes to different areas and alternate routes,
- thickness of windows and portholes,
- types of glass used.

External information such as the following is invaluable as well:

- hull construction;

- height of deck above the water line;

- lighting;

- ropes, bumpers, or ladders on the side of the ship;

- location of open hatches;

- proximity of other boats and whether any of them are providing security for the hostage-takers;

- boarding ramps in place; and

- guards on deck.

INSERTION

Generally, insertion of a rescue team will not be by swimming (although combat swimmers can be invaluable for intelligence gathering: checking the hull of the ship for explosive devices, incapacitating the ship to prevent movement, or, possibly, eliminating sentries on the ship's deck). Insertion will usually be via fast rope from a helicopter or from a small, fast boat. When approaching larger ships, a magnetic pole connection may be used between the assault boat and the ship to aid in the assault. However, there is one school of thought which believes it is much easier to fight down than up; thus if possible to use a comparatively larger vessel to allow an assault team to rope down to the deck of the target vehicle can be used, it is preferred. This is usually only a viable option, however, if the incident it taking place aboard a relatively small craft, such as a yacht. It is far more likely that a boat insertion will be via a Zodiac or other small craft.

AUTHOR'S NOTE

Boats may also be used as a distraction, or as a distraction in conjunction with an insertion. For example, girls in skimpy bikinis or fishermen on the boat can attract attention and conceal swimmers being inserted on the side away from the target craft. Bright spotlights from other ships may also be shone on the deck of the target ship to blind any sentries while an insertion is taking place.

Boarding From Small Boats

When boarding from small boats, normally, the approach will be from the rear very quickly. If such an insertion is to have a high likelihood of success, it is absolutely critical that the operator of the insertion craft be highly competent. Assault teams planning to carry out a boarding of a ship, whether it is stationary or underway, will have to be extremely careful that they do not get mangled fingers during the transfer between the two craft. Such extensive practice is necessary to carry out such assaults, especially on ships which are underway that only the most sophisticated units such as SEAL Team 6 or the SBS have reached a high state of competency.

Fast Rope Insertion

The helicopter fast rope insertion directly onto the deck of the target ship is probably the most desirable insertion method; however, the pilot must be used to maritime operations, as the ship's deck may well be bobbing up and down. If hostage-takers are on deck to contest the insertion, there may also have to be covering fire available either from the helicopter or externally while the assault team is fast-roping down. The trade-off between insertion from a boat or by combat swimmers versus helicopter fast rope is that the two insertion methods directly from the water normally offer more

stealth but are slower, while the fast rope is faster but is also quite likely to attract attention. To allow a fast rope insertion to remain as clandestine as possible, the standard tactic in assaulting a ship at sea is for the helicopter to approach from the rear, flying at wave top, then to flare up just over the fan tail for a rapid fast rope insertion. SEAL Team 6 has practised this manoeuvre so often that six men can fast-rope to the deck from 60 feet in four seconds. Once the insertion is completed, the helicopter quickly veers away.

Combat Swimmers

If combat swimmers will be used either for intelligence gathering or as part of the assault force, there are some special considerations which apply. Although divers will rarely carry out the assault, they may well be committed to the operation in support of the actual assault team. As a result, divers assigned to hostage rescue units must be used to night diving and 'black water' diving in murky or even polluted water.

EXAMPLE

France's GIGN trains its personnel to lie on the bottom of the Seine for extended periods, as barges pass a few feet overhead, to learn the patience and confidence necessary for an underwater infiltration.

Hostage Rescue Unit (HRU) divers will need to be skilled with closed circuit breathing apparatus which does not give off bubbles as they approach a target vessel.

HRU divers will also need specialised equipment, much of it already in the inventory of units such as the SEALs or SBS. For intelligence gathering, underwater cameras such as the Nikonos or underwater video cameras are extremely important. There are also specialised night vision devices for combat swimmers – one of the best from Israel – that are an invaluable intelligence gathering aid.

WEAPONS COMPATIBLE WITH MARITIME USAGE

For any unit tasked with maritime rescue, whether via the surface or from beneath it, weapons and radios which can survive in an ocean environment are critical. Most modern weapons systems and ammunition will hold up to maritime usage; however, for weapons which will be used by combat swimmers, tests of functioning after being submerged and tests of ammunition after exposure to salt water are important. GIGN used to have Norma load special .357 magnum rounds for use in underwater operations. Generally operational ammo will have been proofed to a depth of at least 5 metres. Although weapons will not normally be fired while submerged, Glock does make a special 'sub aqua' version of its Model 17 which is designed for firing underwater. Since most weapons are not intended to fire with water in the barrel, however, it is important that HRUs approaching from the water learn to tilt the barrels of their weapons downward quickly to clear the barrel as they board a target vessel. Some units have special waterproof containers to allow swimming with their weapons. For snipers who will be inserted by swimming or boat, such a container might be invaluable.

Sniping Rifles

It should be noted, though, that there are sniping rifles specifically designed using polymer furniture to hold up to the maritime environment. A scope that will hold up as well is extremely critical.

Leupold makes sniping scopes which are waterproof to at least 30 feet, and these are very popular with units having a maritime hostage rescue mission. Remember, too, that for a ship assault, it is quite possible that snipers will have to reach their shooting positions either by swimming or via boat.

Buoyancy Panels

Another problem for swimmers particularly is the weight of equipment they may have to carry. To help counter this additional weight, the US Navy SEALs have load bearing vests which have built in buoyancy panels to help counteract the weight of ammunition and gear.

Assault Ladders

Assault ladders to be employed for boarding should be padded to dampen noise. If assault ladders are to be emplaced by combat swimmers, then they may need either their own buoyancy or have flotation devices affixed to allow them to be easily towed to the target. Some swimmer units have telescoping ladders with padded hooks to allow them to be placed quickly on a railing or deck lip. Slings for weapons

are absolutely critical so that the hands are free for climbing and so that if the weapon is released it will not fall into the water.

Night Vision Optics

Because boarding may take place in complete darkness or the power may be cut when advancing down passageways, night vision optics will probably be required for a team clearing a ship.

Ammunition

Serious consideration should be given, too, to at least some personnel having rifle calibre weapons with two types of ammunition – frangible and armour piercing.

Since many ships will have steel bulkheads, the danger of ricochet when firing in passageways or compartments where hostages are present makes frangible ammunition desirable.

On the other hand, the possibility exists of needing to take a shot through a bulkhead at a hostage-taker behind cover, in which case armour piercing ammunition would be desirable.

If two types of ammunition are carried, then it is important to colour code the magazines to avoid mistakes. The danger of ricochet or residue from frangible ammo also makes it highly desirable that shipboard clearing teams wear ballistic goggles.

Chemical Munitions

While carrying out the clearing of a ship, chemical munitions may be introduced; however, the ventilation system on many ships may either inhibit or magnify the effects of gas. Consultation with ship designers and maintenance personnel may be advisable if chemical munitions are to be used. Because of the presence of so much steel in the passageways and compartments of ships, the effects of distraction devices may be enhanced slightly due to echo and reverberation.

CLEARING THE SHIP

When clearing stairwells and passageways aboard ships, the SWAT camera or inspection mirror will probably prove invaluable. Some passageways, however, will be so narrow that normal team movement will

probably not be possible. Instead, it may be necessary to have one or two men advance low – in a crouch or maybe even crawling – while others cover them from behind a bulkhead. As passageways are cleared, it will be important, too, that hatches are secured along the route. Dogged steel doors or hatches may be secured using wedges, while naval quick action doors (the type with a spinning wheel) can be tied off to secure them.

The nature of ship construction, however, with watertight doors and numerous passages and hatches, will probably require an extensive clearing effort. As a result, intelligence about the location of hostages and hostage-taker is extremely important. It must be remembered, as well, that the clearing of a ship cannot begin until the assault team is safely aboard. Therefore, the insertion process, whether from the water or from a helicopter, must be carried out successfully. If the insertion is opposed, then having snipers or other shooters in position to give covering fire may well determine success or failure of the entire operation.

CREATING SPECIALISED MARITIME RESCUE UNITS

In many countries, one counterterrorist unit has responsibility for incidents on land, while another has responsibility for those on the water. For example, in the US, the FBI HRT and Delta Force have responsibility for operations on land, while SEAL Team Six has responsibility for incidents at sea. Likewise in the UK, the SAS has responsibility for land, the SBS for operations at sea. Although this necessitates the maintenance and training of two complete units, it also allows the unit, such as SEAL Team 6, tasked with maritime rescues to constantly practise the highly specialised skills needed to carry out a successful rescue aboard a sea-going vessel.

ASSAULTING AN AIRCRAFT

Because of the resources needed to carry out a successful assault on a hijacked airliner, normally only the most highly trained national counterterrorist units are assigned this mission. Nevertheless, the large number of smaller airports served by commuter planes or private aircraft necessitates that every unit charged with hostage rescue give at least some consideration to specialised problems of aircraft assault.

NUMBER OF PERSONNEL

Those teams charged with carrying out operations against large commercial passenger jets feel that as many as 40 personnel may be needed just for the assault. For a 747 this figure could increase to 72 personnel. In addition, snipers/observers, drivers, ladder handlers, negotiators, command personnel, distraction deployers and others will be needed. In at least one major practice assault in the US, almost 100 personnel were eventually involved.

PLANNING THE ASSAULT

The likelihood of a successful assault on an airliner is increased dramatically if pre-planning and practice have taken place. Those teams charged with aircraft assault will normally arrange to practise on each of the major aircraft types in service with flag carrier airlines. It is important for those who will assault an aircraft to know in advance how doors open on each type of aircraft. For example, the 747 and DC-10 have side hinges and swing out, while the 767 has an electronically operated door that opens upwards. The 727 has a door and stair combination allowing exit from the rear. A team which is already aware of these different types of doors and their location and has practised entries through them has a much greater chance of carrying out a successful assault. However, entries are more likely to be carried out through emergency exits over the wings, the cockpit emergency exit, or hatches and cargo doors. Still, pre-knowledge and practice can speed up such entries immeasurably.

Entry and Manoeuvre

Pre-planning and practice will also enable the team to determine possible problem areas. For example, because of the difficulty in entering through the emergency exits over the wing, experienced teams normally assign their smallest operators this task. Practice has also shown that when stealthily moving up a wing prior to an assault, the entry team must step very carefully or they may start

gasoline stored in the wings moving, thus alerting hostage-takers to their presence. France's GIGN has an interesting approach to such entries through emergency exits over the wings. Before any entry men are inserted, trained dogs, who will attack anyone with a weapon in his hands, are first inserted. Despite GIGN's intensive training on aircraft assaults numerous problems have been encountered (see Appendix 1). When planning for the entry, it is best if multiple entry points are used to get as many 'shooters' as possible on to the plane quickly.

Ladders

Having ladders available which are the proper size for each type of aircraft and which are designed to allow a heavily loaded assault team member to ascend quickly is another necessity. At least some national rescue teams have pre-packaged kits of ladders and other entry tools stored for each type of airliner they might have to assault.

Intelligence

Intelligence will also be very important in planning an aircraft assault. Among the information which will be invaluable is the type and size of aircraft, number of passengers and crew, where it is located in the airport and any blind spots, to allow an approach. It is also useful to know if any passengers or law enforcement or military personnel who may try to assist during an assault are on board.

Distraction

When planning the approach to the aircraft, look for any aids to infiltration, such as baggage carts or service vehicles which may be parked nearby. Distraction is important in diverting the attention of the hostage-takers; however, care must be used in deploying distraction devices because of the possibility of fire aboard an aircraft. There are also problems with deploying gas, which is also a fire hazard, but even more importantly, the combination of a gas-filled compartment and panicked passengers will probably make it impossible to locate and neutralise the hostage-takers in a timely manner.

WHEN TO ASSAULT AN AIRCRAFT

Based on actual rescue operations and practice scenarios, it is very difficult to carry out an assault on an aircraft without at least some hostages being injured or killed. The contained nature of the aircraft cabin is such that if a hostage-taker fires any shots, he is likely to hit a hostage. As a result, an aircraft assault should generally only be carried out if it becomes apparent that the hostages are in far more danger if the assault team does not go in than if it does.

Although many police hostage rescue teams will find themselves called upon to deal with incidents in buildings or in vehicles, those incidents which occur aboard ships or aircraft will most likely fall under the jurisdiction of national counterterrorist units. Successful assaults against ships or aircraft require the degree of expertise and assets that only such highly trained, well-funded, full time HRUs can muster.

CHAPTER 11

CONCLUSIONS AND GENERAL PRINCIPLES

When a hostage incident occurs, particularly when it is carried out by terrorists who detain a substantial number of people, not just the hostages themselves are held hostage but the entire system of government within the country where the incident occurs, or of which the hostages are citizens, is also held hostage.

In incidents which cross national boundaries, the entire fabric of world interdependence in matters of foreign nationals and security cooperation is often tested. As a result, massive responsibility rides on the ballistic-vest-clad shoulders of the hostage rescue operator.

PLANNING A SUCCESSFUL RESCUE

In the most professional of units, which train constantly and maintain a ready force 24 hours a day, seven days a week, all of their dedication and hard work may be tested in one incident where they face what is essentially a no-win situation. Even many of the most successful hostage rescue operations ever carried out resulted in the death of one or more hostages. If a unit must 'go in' and ten hostages die, while 150 live, is the mission a success or failure? Certainly, if all 160 hostages would have died had the assault not been launched, then it must considered a success. But, outside the community of those involved in counterterrorism and hostage rescue who realise just how tough a rescue operation is to execute, particularly against a hijacked aircraft, failures or perceived failures often receive much more attention than successes. Not only that, but it is impossible to calculate how many hostage incidents have been avoided because of the knowledge that ready teams from the FBI HRT, the SAS, GIGN or GSG-9 are poised to go into action. Certainly, enlightened self-interest has caused some terrorists to look elsewhere for a target rather than face the highly efficient counterterrorist warriors their actions might launch against them.

THE NEGOTIATED SOLUTION

As good as the best hostage rescue units are, however, the best solution remains negotiating the incident to a conclusion without loss of life. In the case of domestic violence, where a family is held hostage by one of its members, or in a crime gone bad which results in hostages, the negotiated solution is often achievable. In many terrorist incidents, a negotiated settlement is also possible as long as at least some of the terrorists' demands are met. The problem with negotiating with terrorists, however, is one of perception. Most governments view negotiating with terrorists as a sign of weakness which will result in future terrorist incidents of a more heinous nature, and there is some truth in this perception. As a result, as an incident goes on, pressure mounts on a government to take decisive action. In fact, as in some incidents which have taken place in Egypt and Venezuela, killing the terrorists seems to take precedence over saving the hostages (see Appendix 1). It should be pointed out here, too, that from a strictly draconian point of view, if a hostage rescue unit has to stage an assault it is preferable if all of the hostage-takers are eliminated. Not only does this immediately neutralise them as a threat, but it also removes them from the 'game' of terrorism whereby a future incident might be precipitated by their fellow terrorists in an attempt to win their release.

SELECTING THE RESCUE TEAM

The selection of those who carry out hostage rescues requires a balance between finding highly motivated, aggressive operators who must also show a great degree of deliberation in their actions. As a result, members of hostage rescue units will normally be more mature than those of other elite police or military organisations. Men who are in their early thirties but in fine physical condition often make excellent choices. Because of the precision shooting skills necessary to carry out successful hostage rescues, marksmanship must remain one of the absolutely critical criteria in selecting members of an HRU. Marksmanship skills can indeed be enhanced through training, but the basic skills must be there. It takes a lot of practice and a lot of confidence in one's ability to be willing to take a shot which will pass within inches of a hostage in order to save that hostage.

TIME

It must also be borne in mind that time is a critical element for those involved in hostage rescue. In the case of a hostage incident which is ongoing, then time is normally on the side of the hostage rescue team, because it allows the negotiator to, perhaps, win concessions, for a bond to grow between hostage-takers and hostages, and for the assault teams constantly to improve their plan and practise for an entry. Once that entry starts, however, time becomes the enemy. Once an entry begins with the deployment of distraction devices, then the team normally has, at most, seven seconds in which to enter and neutralise the hostage-takers. After that, the odds that hostages will die increase dramatically.

DISTRACTION

Anything which can gain seconds by diverting the hostage-taker is 'golden time' for the rescue team. In every training scenario involving hostages, the assault team and the other members of the rescue team should incorporate distraction. Negotiators, too, should practise ploys for distracting a subject from a potential entry. A famous early American baseball player named 'Wee Willie' Keeler once explained his philosophy of hitting as, 'I hit 'em where they ain't!' He could have been explaining hostage rescue tactics as well.

ASSEMBLING DATA

To hit the hostage-takers where they 'ain't', though, requires timely and valid intelligence. As a result, the snipers, negotiators and intelligence specialists must assemble as much data about the site, hostage-takers and hostages as possible. Only with information – particularly about the location of the hostages and hostage-takers – can an assault plan with a reasonable chance of success be implemented.

Hostage rescue is a very serious business with very little margin for error. That's why even the most elite military or police units when assigned this mission must go through months, even years, of additional training and must constantly continue that training so their skills remain sharp. The tactics and techniques discussed in this book are drawn from the experiences of the author and hundreds of others from whom he has learned. Nevertheless, these remain general precepts. Each hostage incident will remain unique and will require a unique solution. However, many elements of that incident may well have occurred before. It's not incidental that most top hostage rescue units consider intelligence to be as important as physical prowess in selecting team members.

By studying incidents that have happened before, perhaps even reconstructing them or variations of them for training, those who must plan and execute a hostage rescue will have a sound basis for creating and implementing their rescue plan.

APPENDIX 1

SYNOPSIS OF ACTUAL INCIDENTS CITED IN THE TEXT

CHAPTER 1

Princes Gate. On 30 April 1980, six terrorists from the Democratic Front for the Liberation of Arabistan took over the Iranian embassy in London, gaining 26 hostages in the process. Five hostages were released during the siege and one was executed. The latter incident precipitated an assault on 5 May by the SAS which had been standing by. Five of the terrorists were killed, while one hostage died and two others were wounded. The televisation of this assault catapulted the SAS and hostage rescue units in general into the spotlight.

CHAPTER 3

South Moluccan Terrorists/ Depunt train incident. On 23 May 1977, nine South Moluccan terrorists seized the Depunt train carrying 94 passengers, while at the same time four of their associates seized the Bovensmilde school containing 105 children and four teachers. The terrorists wanted Holland to force Indonesia to grant independence to the island of South Molucca to give the expatriate population a homeland. Having traditionally served in the Dutch army, they had to leave Indonesia when it gained independence from Holland. The incident dragged on for three weeks, partially at least because the terrorists viewed the Dutch government as soft and unwilling to use force, thus depriving the negotiators of 'teeth'. Finally, the Royal Dutch Marines assaulted both venues simultaneously, killing six terrorists on the train, with the loss of two hostages. All terrorists at the school were taken alive and the hostages were all rescued. Among the interesting aspects of this assault was the use of the Royal Dutch Air Force, which flew low and kicked in their afterburners over the train as a distraction to force the terrorists and hostages to 'duck' during the assault.

CHAPTER 5
Branch Davidian Compound.

The Bureau of Alcohol, Tobacco and Firearms (BATF) raided this religious compound on 28 February 1993. Agents from the BATF were killed and a siege, which lasted about a month, ensued. Although some negotiators advised against an assault, in May 1993 an attempt by FBI agents to insert tear gas resulted in a fire – allegedly set by those in the compound – which resulted in the death of 75 Branch Davidians, including 33 women and children. A counter-argument places the blame for the fire with the deployment of chemical munitions and tear gas against the compound. This incident caused the FBI to re-evaluate its negotiation policies and decision-making techniques at barricade/hostage situations. There is some controversy about whether this should be classed as a barricade or hostage situation, as the Justice Department operated on the assumption that children within the compound were hostages.

Rescue of General Dozier. In January 1982, ten members of the Italian NOCS *(Nucleo Operativo di Centrale di Sicurezza* – Central Security Operations Group) carried out a rescue of kidnapped US General James Dozier, the highest ranking US officer in Italy, who was being held by members of the Red Brigade. During the rescue, the ten members of NOCS (normally pronounced 'knocks' in the counterterrorist community) felled the terrorists with martial arts techniques and captured them for trial.

CHAPTER 6

Lima. On 18 December 1996, 14 Marxist Tupac Amaru rebels seized the Japanese Ambassador's residence in Lima, Peru, while a party with 600 guests was underway. The rebels stated that they had seized the residence to protest against Japanese interference in the political life of Peru (the President of Peru is of Japanese descent) and also to protest treatment of members of their group in prison. Within the first two weeks all but 74 hostages were released, but the incident dragged on for over four months. Peruvian counterterrorist personnel had managed to place cameras and listening devices which allowed them to glean excellent intelligence about the terrorists' routine. The fact the siege lasted so long also allowed intensive training on a mock-up of the residence and gave the rescue team time to construct a 220 metre tunnel ten metres beneath the ground for the insertion of an assault team. The rescue was launched on 22 April 1997 and was so carefully rehearsed that it was over within 41 seconds from the beginning of the assault. In the process two Peruvian commandos were killed, as was one hostage. All 14 terrorists died in the assault.

CHAPTER 8
Littleton, Colorado. On 20 April 1999 at Columbine High School in Littleton, Colorado, two teenagers armed with firearms and home-made bombs killed twelve classmates and one teacher and wounded at least 20 others before killing themselves. This incident led law-enforcement agencies throughout the US to re-evaluate their policies for dealing with 'active shooters' and provided an impetus to agencies tasked with rescues and entries to practise operations at schools.

Ma'alot. On 14 May 1974 three Palestinian terrorists took 100 hostages at a school in Ma'alot, Israel. Sayeret Mat'kal (an Israeli counterterrorist unit) attempted an assault but hesitated too long and acted on bad intelligence (they misjudged the location of the terrorists in the building). 26 hostages were killed and 60 badly wounded. As a result of this incident, Israel formed the Ya'ma'n counterterrorist units.

CHAPTER 9
Djibouti. In February 1976, six terrorists from the Front for the Liberation of the Coast of Somalia hijacked a school bus carrying children of French Air Force personnel. They took the bus to the Djibouti/Somalia border where they could be covered by Somali border

guards who were sympathetic to their cause. The commander of GIGN and nine unit members were deployed for a rescue. Because the bus was parked in the open it was deemed best to eliminate the hostage-takers with sniper-fire if possible. To prevent the children from presenting silhouettes which might obscure a shot at the terrorists, drugged food was sent to the bus, resulting in the children falling asleep. When the 'green light' was given, five of the six terrorists were eliminated with precision shots, but one was not on the bus. He managed to rush back and kill one girl before the GIGN operators could charge the 200 metres between their position and the bus to eliminate him. All other hostages were safely rescued.

Munich. On 5 September 1972, eight terrorists from Black September attacked the quarters of Israel's Olympic team, taking nine men hostage and killing two men who resisted to allow eleven others to escape. (Black September was formed in response to grievances against the Jordanian treatment of Palestinians living in Jordan. The logic of then targeting Israel is hard to grasp!) The terrorists demanded the release of 200 terrorists held in Israel and other countries. Eventually, the terrorists were told they would be given a plane and were taken, along with their hostages, to the airport, where German police planned to stop them with four snipers (at best a quarter of the number which would normally have been considered sufficient by a trained hostage rescue unit). There was also no assault team ready to follow-up should the snipers fail to neutralise all the terrorists. In the resulting fiasco, all the hostages and five of the terrorists died. The other three terrorists were captured. This incident was the impetus for the formation of GSG-9 and many other specialised counterterrorist units.

CHAPTER 10
Entebbe. On 27 June 1976 an Air France plane was hijacked by a combination of PLO and Baader-Meinhof terrorists and forced to land at Entebbe Airport in Uganda. Various terrorist groups formed alliances of

sorts in the 1970s based on shared Marxist beliefs and the practicality that security forces might not be looking for Westerners in the Middle East, etc. (Baader-Meinhof was the principal German terrorist group at this time.) The Germans attracted less attention on a flight to Israel than obvious Middle Eastern types. 103 Jewish and Israeli hostages were separated and kept by the hostage-takers so that anyone executed would have a direct effect on Israel. The Ugandan dictator Idi Amin was supporting the terrorists and using his soldiers to provide additional security, making a rescue extremely difficult. Nevertheless, the Israelis deployed a combined force of Sayeret Mat'kal and paratroopers to launch a rescue. After an eight-hour flight, the Israeli strike force landed at Entebbe in three Hercules aircraft. The rescue was carried out by using a fake Idi Amin as a ruse to get near the terminal (they used an identical limo and counted on the fact he inspired such fear in his troops that no-one would want to get too close). Three hostages were killed and one woman hostage who was in hospital at the time later 'disappeared' and is assumed to have been killed. All of the remaining hostages were rescued. At least 20 Ugandan soldiers as well as the terrorist guards were killed and numerous Ugandan soldiers were wounded. The Israeli casualty was 'Yoni' Netanyahu, the leader of the operation and brother of Benjamin Netanyahu.

Mogidishu. On 13 October 1977, four Arab terrorists acting as surrogates for the German terrorists Baader-Meinhof, hijacked a Lufthansa jet in an attempt to gain the release of Baader-Meinhof terrorists. (For an explanation of terrorist alliances see Entebbe.) The plane finally landed at Mogidishu, Somalia. The pilot, who had been passing information via the radio, was killed. A 20-man GSG-9 assault force, along with two members of the SAS who had supplied stun grenades, was deployed. Using the stun grenades as a distraction to draw the terrorists to the front of the plane, GSG-9 assaulted, freeing all 86 hostages and killing or capturing all four terrorists.

Marseilles Aircraft Assault. In December 1994 an Air France flight was hijacked in Algeria by four terrorists from the Armed Islamic Group, a very militant fundamentalist organisation. Two days after it was seized, the plane was flown, with 172 passengers aboard, to Marseilles. The few elderly hostages who were released mentioned the erratic behaviour of the terrorists and their constant references to paradise. Therefore, when the hostages asked for the plane to be refuelled so that they could fly to Paris and stopped communicating, it was decided it was quite likely that they planned to crash the plane into the French capital. As a result, GIGN was authorised to assault the aircraft. GIGN had snipers positioned in the control tower to cover the cockpit, while 40 men were available for the assault. Members of the assault team had infiltrated near the aircraft wearing the uniforms of airport services personnel. The plan called for 15 men to enter after climbing a mobile stairway positioned by the right front door of the aircraft. When the snipers spotted all four

terrorists in the cockpit, or near it, an attempt was made to hurl a distraction device through a cockpit window, but a problem was encounted when a terrorist threw a grenade. A device was successfully thrown through the window on a second attempt. The assault force, however, encountered difficulties getting through the door. They quickly began clearing the aircraft as they had rehearsed on a similar model, eventually containing the terrorists in the cockpit where they continued to fire at the passengers and GIGN operators. Eventually all four terrorists were killed, while 13 passengers, three crew members and nine GIGN operators were injured.

CHAPTER 11
Egyptian Aircraft Rescue Attempt. Egypt's Force 777 has been involved in two disastrous aircraft assaults, both of which can act as text book cases on how not to run a rescue operation. The first occurred on 18 February 1978, when a Cyprus Airways jet bound for Cairo and carrying many Egyptian passengers

was hijacked and parked on the ground at Nicosia airport. Without receiving the permission of Cypriot authorities, Force 777 landed and immediately attempted an assault, resulting in a fire-fight with Cypriot National Guardsmen securing the aircraft, who believed the Egyptians to be additional terrorists reinforcing those already on the plane. In the resulting fire-fight, 15 Force 777 Commandos were killed and others wounded. Numerous Cypriot National Guardsmen were also killed. The plane was not assaulted.

The second attempt occurred on 24 November 1985, when terrorists from the Abu Nidal faction hijacked an Egyptair flight in Athens and took it to Malta. (Abu Nidal was a Palestinian terrorist who masterminded terrorist operations in the 1980s, including this hijacking.) This time Force 777 did have permission from the Maltese government to carry out a rescue. However, in attempting an explosive entry, almost 20 hostages were killed in the blast. The assault team then threw smoke grenades which

obscured their vision and created panic in the aircraft. So intent were the commandos on killing the terrorists that they fired at anything they saw moving in the aisles, blindly killing more hostages in the process. Force 777 snipers then killed additional hostages attempting to escape from the aircraft. In total, 57 hostages died during the operation.

Venezuelan Aircraft Assault. In July 1984, the Venezuelan Special Intervention Brigade carried out an assault against a hijacked aircraft at Aruba. All 79 passengers were rescued in the assault, but there are indications that the assault was primarily launched to silence the hostage-takers, who were allegedly demanding payment for covert operations they had carried out for the government.

APPENDIX 2

Data Sheet – **HOSTAGE-TAKER**

Name _____ Sex: M or F

Age _____ Race _____ Hair _____

Eyes _____ Height _____ Weight _____

Clothing _____

Weapons & Body Armour _____

Medical History _____

Photo

If

Available

_____

Psychiatric History _____

Prescription Medications Used _____

Drug and Alcohol Abuse _____

Criminal Record _____

Propensity Towards Violence _____

Military or Police Experience (especially with weapons or explosives)

_____

Marital Status _____ Bitter Divorce? _____

Close Relatives _____

Affiliation with Gangs or Extremist Groups _____

Employed or Unemployed _____ If employed, where? _____

Education _____

Hobbies and Interests _____

Other Info of Possible Importance _____

Data Sheet – **HOSTAGE**

Name _____ Sex: M or F

Age _____ Race _____ Hair _____

Eyes _____ Height _____ Weight _____

Clothing _____

Circumstances in which taken hostage

_____

Photo

If

Available

Was this hostage targeted or was he/she taken randomly?
_____

Medical Problems (especially those such as heart trouble which might impact a rescue attempt)
_____

Prescription Medications Used
_____

Marital Status _____ Are family members being held also?_____

If so, who and what relationship?
_____

Other Close Relatives
_____

Employer _____ Education _____

Hobbies and Interests _____

Psychological evaluation _____
_____

Negotiator's notes if contact is made with hostage
_____

Other Info of Possible Importance _____

APPENDIX 3

HOSTAGE NEGOTIATOR'S PSYCHOLOGICAL CHECK LIST

(To be used in conjunction with the team's psychologist)

Schizophrenia
Indicators:

– Subject is delusional (especially bizarre delusions).   ____

– Subject suffers from hallucinations.   ____

– Subject's speech and behavior are disorganized.   ____

– Subject displays a limited range of emotional expression.   ____

– Subject displays a loss of fluency in thought and speech.   ____

– Subject presents inappropriate reactions.   ____

Implications for the hostage rescue team:

The suspect who is schizophrenic will become depersonalised, making it less likely he will develop a bond with hostages. He may also become phobic and display extreme anxiety making it difficult for the negotiator to gain his confidence. Some schizophrenics will have a substantially greater predisposition towards violence.

Paranoid Schizophrenia

The paranoid schizophrenic will display many of the characteristics of the schizophrenic but will not normally show the same level of disorganisation. Other indicators include:

– Anxiety   ____

– Anger   ____

– Aloofness   ____

– Argumentativeness   ____

– Auditory delusions (especially those which tell him to take certain actions). ____

– Feelings of persecution ____

Implications:

The paranoid schizophrenic is often very intelligent but displays a propensity towards violence and suicide.

Bipolar Disorder

Indicators when in a manic phase:
– The subject is so restless he cannot sit still. ____

– The subject cannot concentrate. ____

– The subject shows rapid, disconnected thoughts and speech. ____

– The subject shows extreme concern with religion in thoughts and speech. ____

– The subject is impulsive. ____

– The subject shows grandiose delusions. ____

– The subject is hyperactive. ____

Indicators when in a depressed phase:
– The subject shows a distinct loss of energy. ____

– The subject shows a lack of interest. ____

– The subject is self-reproachful. ____

– The subject is suicidal.

____

Implications for the hostage rescue team:

During the manic phase, the subject might kill the hostages on impulse. He may also fail to grasp the threat posed by the authorities on the scene and, thus, not show the usual inhibitions against violence or willingness to negotiate. In the depressive stage, the subject may tell the negotiator to 'go away' or otherwise refuse to communicate.

Substance-Induced Psychotic Disorders

This type will share indicators with other psychotic personalities but some specific indicators are:

– The subject has a history of substance abuse.   ———

– The subject suffers hallucinations (particularly if he does not realise they are caused by alcohol or drugs).   ———

– The subject suffers delusions.   ———

Implications:

Subjects suffering substance-related psychotic symptoms are prone to delusions of persecution. They may also see faces distorted, offering potential for viewing the hostages as monsters or other aberrations. This could precipitate violence against the hostages.

Antisocial Personality (Sociopathy)

Indicators:

– The subject shows little or no sense of responsibility/tends to blame others.   ———

– The subject shows disregard for the truth.   ———

– The subject exhibits no sense of shame.   ———

– The subject displays anti-social behaviour without regret.   ———

– The subject does not learn from experience.   ———

– The subject shows poor insight.   ———

– The subject does not respond to kindness.   ———

– The subject is selfish and callous.   ———

– The subject has a low frustration tolerance.   ———

–The subject is pragmatic and realistic in dealing with the negotiator.   ———

NOTE: Some of these indicators may be gleaned from a prior criminal record as this psychological type has very likely had previous problems with the authorities.

Implications for the hostage rescue team:

Although this type will have little regard for laws or social conventions, nor for the hostages, he will have a high regard for himself. As a result, self-preservation will be a motivator and the knowledge that an entry team is on site will give him strong incentive to negotiate the best deal he can.

Inadequate Personality

Indicators:

–Subject has difficulty responding to emotional, social, intellectual, or physical demands.

–Subject relies on others for ideas or opinions. ___

–Subject is inept in dealing with details. ___

–Subject shows social instability. ___

–Subject shows poor judgment. ___

–Subject lacks stamina. ___

–Subject shows prolonged unreasonableness. ___

Implications:

This type of personality may prove hard to engage in negotiations and will probably be unable to make decisions. If there is more than one hostage-taker, it would be better not to negotiate with this individual, who is more likely to be a follower than a leader. However, there may be circumstances where an especially skilful negotiator can exert influence over this personality type.

RECOMMENDED READING

Beckwith, C., *Delta Force* (NY: Harcourt, Brace, Janovitch, 1983)

Davies, B., *Fire Magic: Hijack at Mogadishu* (London: Bloomsbury, 1994)

Dobson, C. and R. Payne, *Counterattack: The West's Battle Against Terrorists* (NY: Facts on File, 1982)

Dobson, C. and R. Payne, *The Terrorists: Their Weapons, Leaders and Tactics* (NY: Facts on File, 1982)

Katz, S.M., *The Illustrated Guide to the World's Top Counterterrorist Forces* (Hong Kong: Concord Publications, 1995)

Katz, S.M., *The Illustrated Guide to the World's Top Naval Special Warfare Units* (Hong Kong: Concord Publications, 2000)

Marcinko, R., *Rogue Warrior* (NY: Pocket Star Books, 1992)

MSCPAC Shipboard Physical Security Training Manual (Oakland, CA: MSCPAC, 1986)

Mattoon, S., *SWAT Training and Employment* (Boulder, CO: Paladin Press, 1987)

Mattoon, S., *Explosive Entry Techniques for Tactical Teams* (Olympia, WA: The Final Option, 1989)

Mattoon, S., *SRT/SWAT Advanced Course* (Olympia, WA: The Final Option, 1989)

Plaster, Maj. J., *The Ultimate Sniper* (Boulder, CO: Paladin Press, 1993)

Sniper Data Book (Olympia, WA: The Final Option, 1991)

Snow, R., SWAT Teams: *Explosive Face-Offs with America's Deadliest Criminals* (NY: Plenum Books, 1996)

Tactical Training Reference Manual, (Washington DC: Office of Nuclear Material Safety and Safeguards, 1988)

Thompson, L., *The Rescuers: The World's Top Counterterrorist Units* (Boulder, CO: Paladin Press, 1986)

US Army Counterterrorism Manual (Sims, AR: Lancer Militaria, 1994)

NOTE: Any reader of this work who is a member of a military or police hostage rescue unit and needs additional information on incidents, equipment, or tactics discussed in this work may contact the author at:

Leroy Thompson
P.O. Box 1739
Manchester, MO 63011
USA

Please include a photocopy of police or military identification and a request on official letterhead. Also, include an e-mail address for a reply.

INDEX